HOW TO BECOME A SUCCESSFUL TRADER

Financial markets, Trading, Scalping, Day-Trading: the immersive guide 2.0

Edition: JDH Éditions
77600 Bussy-Saint-Georges. France
Printed by BoD - Books on Demand, Norderstedt, Germany

ISBN: 978-2-38127-199-6
Legal deposit: October 2021

HOW TO BECOME A SUCCESSFUL TRADER

Financial markets, Trading, Scalping, Day-Trading: the immersive guide 2.0

With Benoist Rousseau

Become a trader on your own account

Founder of the Andlil.co.uk website

JDH Éditions

Les Pros de l'Éco

Translated by: Louise Taylor

"Les Pros de l'Éco" Collection

Directed by Jean-David Haddad

This collection ensembles writings from economics professionals, intended for the general public. These professionals highlight particular knowledge about an issue or their research results, in an educational and accessible way.

The various books are unique and are not interchangeable with more "academic" books.

Instructions for reading a QR code on your Smartphone / Tablet

1) Open the Camera application

2) Point the camera lens at the QR code to be scanned

3) Wait for 2 to 3 seconds without pressing the shutter button

4) A notification will appear at the top of the screen. Then simply click on the notification to display the QR code's content.

5) If no notification appears, download a QR code application. This takes a few seconds. Then use it to read the QR codes.

You can consult the private content and unpublished videos that are extension of the book by connecting to the site

https://www.andlil.co.uk/book/

This book is dedicated to Arnaud, Cynthia, Daniel, Damien, Florian, Gérard, Jean-David, Marie, Marius, Renée, unfailing, patient friends who have always supported and encouraged me in my craziest projects.

A word from the Author

If you have your hands on this book it's because you are passionate about financial markets, that you aspire to improve your trading and, perhaps, one day become a trader on your own account.

With this book, I would like to share my 25 years of trading experience with you so that you don't make the same mistakes as I did and spend too many years going around in circles and losing money as I did.

It aims to warn you of the dangers and difficulties that await you on the road to trading, the inevitable challenges and the profound changes that will have to be accepted and made in order to progress. Of course, I will explain my trading method and, more specifically, how I do scalping.

But my way of trading is only there to serve as an illustrative example and not as an example to be followed blindly. You will have to find your own way, look for your personal method because trading is, above all, tailor-made and not ready-to-wear.

You will not get anywhere by trying to copy, imitate or mimic another trader. At best, you will waste time and money trying to fit into his shoes when they are not your size, at worst you will get discouraged and become bitter. "Why does he succeed at trading and I don't?" Well, simply because you're not him and he is trading in his own way and not someone else's.

This trader, whoever he is, can at best be an inspiration to you, but you will inevitably have to change, modify and remodel his trading method to make it a unique new method: yours.

Accept the idea of your uniqueness and that your way of trading must become unique. It must be part of you, with your personality and your psychology. The good news is that we're not clones!

One day you will manage to trade without asking yourself (too many) questions, in a natural, fluid, stress-free way regardless of volatility. You will remain calm when others panic, you will remain calm when others are euphoric. You will become your own master, you will control your emotions, you will limit your flaws and you will amplify your qualities. Doesn't that sound great?

But for that to happen, to become free in the literal and figurative sense, you will have to search, persevere and suffer.

No one can do this work for you, no one can give you miracle solutions or methods, there is no Holy Grail for trading. I won't be the one to throw the first stone at you if you look for "the miracle", I have spent more than a decade on that illusory quest. If I can save you 10 years of wandering, that'll be a good kick start.

I know that in a society where immediacy and very little effort have been elevated to the rank of idols, you will not be thrilled with my pep talk. If you are looking for an easy route where you get everything quickly, this book is not for you. There is no miracle. If you are willing to question yourself and really work on your trading and on yourself, I hope this book will help you do so.

To encourage you to become autonomous and find your own way, this book has the distinctive characteristic of being an immersive and dynamic guide, that is to say, it combines writing, images, videos and speech. It is only a gateway to a larger and evolving world.

This book gives you access to a private area of the www.Andlil.co.uk site.

This private section is an essential complement to this book, to help you progress step by step.

You will find all the information you need to access this private, personal and evolving area:

https://www.andlil.co.uk/book/

I would like to end on a positive note: by embarking on trading, even if it means searching, persevering and suffering, you are embarking on a real journey that can be wonderful.

Have a good read and good work!

Benoist Rousseau

THE BASICS OF TRADING

THE START OF THE JOURNEY

1

TRADER, IT'S A PROFESSION

It may be strange to state this obvious fact, but being a trader is a profession. A real profession. A difficult, demanding profession that requires discipline, high resistance to stress, skilled analysis and adaptation, outstanding psychology, self-control, etc. and living with a sword of Damocles hanging over your head and enjoying it, or at least accepting living with this threat.

Being a trader on your own account is like being a Michelin-starred chef in a top restaurant, there is no room for error.

I've had a lot of discussions with numerous Michelin-starred chefs and all of them have one thing in common
with a trader: the pressure to keep their stars. Making mistakes costs them dearly. If, in the course of a year, during one single day, they send out dishes that are not perfect, and if,

through misfortune, there is a restaurant guide inspector at the table, they may lose their stars.

Their status and rank are only temporary, nothing is definitive. A Michelin-starred chef can crash and fall into the anonymity of the Yellow Pages rather than remain in the Red Guide.

It's the same with trading. It's a constant struggle to remain at the high requirement levels that the profession demands. However, we are more fortunate than a top Michelin-starred chef because, if we have effective money management, we can afford to make mistakes during our trading year. Our money management is our lifeline!

On the other hand, an athlete might only be a champion once in his life but he remains a champion until he dies. If he won the Olympic Games gold medal for boxing in the lightweight category at 20 years old, he will be that champion for his whole life, even at 80 years old when he weighs 150 kg. He's a champion, he'll always be a champion!

A trader, even if he has many similarities with a top athlete, has no such luck. He has to train, adapt and progress throughout his life. There is nothing more Darwinian than trading, it is permanent adaptation and that is what makes it so appealing.

If you imagine a trader as a Wall Street wolf (who is not a trader by the way, but more a cold calling soap salesman), you are seriously off track.
Completely forget Hollywood fairy tales of excitement, drugs and everything that goes with it. A trader on his own account

is, above all, during his trading sessions, a seventh level Zen monk. Calm and concentrated. I know, it's not sexy.

Totally forget the advertising of quick and easy financial gains with a Ferrari, a yacht and a pretty little blonde on your arm. I know, it's difficult.

Totally forget the miracle training courses on a 3-page PDF or the £500 trading robots that will make you a millionaire within a year. I know, it's unfortunate.

Like any profession, trading requires a long period of training. Becoming a baker and finishing an apprenticeship takes one to three years. Becoming a qualified teacher takes at least four years. To become a lawyer, doctor, surgeon, etc. can take up to between 7 to 10 years.

And to become a trader, one of the most difficult professions in the world, how many years does that take?

The answer is specific to each person, as in any profession there are talented people, there are people who have not been blessed with natural talent, but who are hard-working and successful, there are dabblers, there are stubborn people who do not want to question themselves because they are right all the time contrary to the market, even if their results obviously do not support their viewpoint, etc.

Personally, I wasted more than a decade looking for a miracle method, a Grail, etc. before I realized that the problem was not the method, but myself.

You really need to absorb this intellectual approach: I'm going to learn a new profession. I'm going back into an apprenticeship, this is no game. I'm getting into this with my innate qualities, which will be useful or not and my weaknesses, which will be pejorative or not, for my trading activity.

Unfortunately, this is why a large proportion of apprentice traders fail. They get into it with myths of fast, easy and effortless money. All you have to do is click. Unfortunately, it's a little more complicated than that.

And that brings us to a question that could be disturbing: can everyone learn to trade?

2

IS TRADING INNATE OR CAN IT BE LEARNED?

Let's look at an experiment that was conducted in the United States in the 1980s to answer this serious question.

It all began when speculator Richard Dennis disagreed with his business partner William Eckhardt. Their dispute revolved around the following question: can trading be taught or do you have to have innate skills?

Richard Denis, the "Prince of the Pit", argued that he could teach trading, while his friend upheld that the success of a trader depends on innate factors (genetically inherited, natural gift, etc.).

They, therefore, agreed to set up a real experiment, with the aim of confirming the accuracy of their respective reasoning through this procedure's results.

They selected 13 apprentices not related to the world of finance and having no particular knowledge of the world of financial markets.

These apprentices were nicknamed "Turtles", Richard Dennis having drawn a parallel with a turtle farm he had visited in Singapore a short time earlier. The Turtle experiment was launched.

I'll skip the details of the method used and go straight to the conclusion. This experiment succeeded far beyond Richard Dennis' expectations. These apprentices made average gains of 80% over the next four years. Some even decided to pursue a career in finance.

So, here was proof that trading can be learned. Good news for everyone: that is the purpose of this book.

Of course, you have to take into consideration what we personally bring to our trading, qualities which support it (patience, innate respect of the rules, etc.) and weaknesses that need correcting, which impair it (impatience, ego, etc.).

One thing that could be criticized in this experiment: the 13 Turtles were selected in advance from more than 1,000 candidates. These were not people chosen at random, there was a pre-selection filter created by Richard Dennis.

But I like to hold onto the main concept: you can learn to trade, it's not just for the elite, for super men or for people who have had outstanding education in the world of finance.

Personally, I only studied economic history and became a humble history teacher for 10 years before deciding to become a trader on my own account.

The only thing that has driven me over the years is my passion for trading. It may be the only 'little something extra' I had over others. Without passion, I don't think anything is possible, in any case nothing has any appeal.

Are you passionate about trading?

All right, come on, let's get to it.

Now let's have a look at how to start learning to trade?

3

THE IMPORTANCE OF PAPER TRADING WHEN YOU BEGIN

Paper Trading is an essential step in learning how to trade. It is absolutely essential for apprentice traders or traders who are changing trading platforms. It enables you to get to grips with the trading interface and to make mistakes without suffering the consequences.

The easiest way is to open a demo account which can be done in 2 clicks. Use a broker who is known to be reliable. Then take advantage of the free, real-time data feeds to get used to it.

Using the QR code below, you can open a free demo account with my broker. This will enable you to follow explanations on my trading method, in the next chapter, more efficiently as you will have the same scalping interface in front of you and real-time prices:

Paper Trading, therefore, consists in simulating purchases and sales of financial instruments (shares, warrants, futures, etc.), but without paying a penny. And, of course, without making any money, it is all hypothetical.

Anecdote
I have heard that there are people who have asked brokers to transfer their virtual earnings from their demo account to their bank account. When the broker refused to convert their virtual gains into real ones, they got angry. I don't know whether to laugh or cry about this.

For older people like me who started trading before the Internet came along, we used to follow stock prices in newspapers or on the radio. I started like that, recording on graph paper prices of the indices I had virtually bought until I had saved enough to be able to trade (using Minitel (a home terminal for the French telecommunications system) of course). Now you can take advantage of the significant convenience of training accounts that give you real-world conditions.

You can, therefore, practice Paper Trading for months. That is to say, you can learn how to trade technically, even if you do not yet have enough capital to trade with.

Paper Trading is therefore used to familiarize yourself, free of charge and without losses, using financial market mechanisms. This is an INDISPENSABLE step for novice traders.

Even for experienced traders, it is really beneficial, because you learn to master the order placement interface, configure your charts, etc. without mistakes costing you money. This step is often overlooked, but you have to know the trading software used, learn to place your buy and sell orders correctly, etc. because if you don't really know your interface, in a real situation, under stress, it is not uncommon at first to make stupid mistakes (buy 10 shares instead of 100, sell instead of buy, etc.).

This may sound crazy to you, but it sometimes happens to experienced traders (I speak from sad experience). So, even if you are a pro, if you change your trading interface, don't skip this step.

However, Paper Trading has two major flaws, it is only a pale imitation of real trading and it is frustrating.

It lacks what makes trading appealing and difficult, reality, i.e. affects and stress. If you lose whilst Paper Trading, it's not a big deal, it doesn't affect you, you don't experience anxiety. You simply start again.

For real trading it's another story, when you lose or gain, you are affected by feelings such as fear, greed, doubt, excitement, etc. that can disrupt your trading enormously.

That is why I recommend that you be as efficient as possible when learning, so as to get as close as possible to the conditions you will face in real life. If you are considering trading with £10,000, it is pointless to credit your demo account with £100,000. This will do more harm than good, we do not trade the same way with £10,000 as with £100,000.

Keep in mind
Your Paper Trading results are not a reflection of your real trading results at all. You are playing a realistic video game, but you don't experience the reality of real-life trading. 90% of your results come from your psychology. With a demo account, you only work on 10% of the whole, the technical aspect. I have known demo traders who had fabulous results for months and months, some of them for several years, and who collapsed with a real account within 72 hours. Just because you are virtually good at a driving video game doesn't mean you can drive a Formula 1 racing car. Just because you're good at a war game on your console doesn't mean you'll react like a veteran soldier if one day live bullets whistle past your ears.

Paper Trading is still very frustrating and it is very difficult psychologically to make virtual gains. Inevitably, you would like to have the £2,200 of virtual earnings, which you made during the week, in your account. We then tend to get angry and move too quickly to real trading, because we feel like we've actually lost £2,200! No, you've gained a little experience without any risk.

When should you switch to real trading? There is no single answer. When you are comfortable, a little more confident in your trading, etc. If you tend to overestimate yourself, keep trading a little, if you are a hesitant individual (a good trader must be hesitant if he wants to survive) don't spend weeks doing Paper Trading either, you will end up going round in circles. I am sidestepping the question, I know.

However, I advise you not to drag your heels for months, or even years, with a demo account. This can be harmful, because you can develop bad habits, such as trading virtually with amounts that you don't initially have in real money. Too many demos kill the trader.

If possible, start trading after establishing your trading method and having a good command of the order placement interface, with a minimal amount that you can lose without any worries and without any regret. (Think of it as the price you pay for your training).

With £1,000 you can start trading Futures in micro lots for example. You will then begin to realize that trading is much more complex than you might think in the early days. All of a sudden, you will have intense emotions that you never felt with a demo account. All your work in the coming months and years will be to understand, channel and educate all those impulses, which are just waiting to emerge, so as to be capable of trading in the same relaxed manner that you had using a demo account.

After a few hours of real trading, you will understand what I am trying to tell you. The real work begins then.

4

THE IMPORTANCE OF TRADING JOURNALS

Keeping a trading journal is an essential step in progressing in trading for both novice and experienced traders.

What is a trading journal? It is a private or open journal where you can record your trading results, impressions, benchmarks, questions, etc. but most importantly, you try to get some perspective over your trading operations.

Effectively, when you are in the heat of the action, you don't have the ability to rise above the occasion and patiently analyse your trades. Only a trading journal enables you to take stock at the end of the day and rate each of your trades according to adherence to your money management rules and personal trading techniques.

After a day of trading, it may sometimes seem tedious, but it is very effective if painstaking work. It is a valuable tool for self-knowledge and it enables you to spot obviously recurring trading mistakes. However, they won't be obvious to you without the journal.

Your trading journal should be seen as a tool that enables you to analyse your trading. It therefore contains essential information that impacts your trading style, your financial market results, etc.

For example, in my trading journal, I record different things each day, assigning them a score out of 10:

How tired I am, my psychological state and each of my trades is noted as it occurs.

This shows, for example:

Monday, 28th October
===
Fatigue: 3/10, I only had four hours sleep last night.
Psychology: 7/10, good morale
Preparation: 10/10 (chart + stock market calendar analysis)
===
Trade 1: good 7/10 RAS
Trade 2: taken too early in anticipation, taken above the support 5/10
Trade 3: no technical reason 2/10
Trade 4: trade out of boredom 0/10
Trade 5: bad conditions, I was on the phone, 3/10

Trade 6: 7/10 classical rebound S2 M, purchase under resale. Possibility to exit better, sold in advance when the 100 tick chart was good.
Etc.

Overall: Overall score of the day: 6/10, not enough sleep => trades of average quality. Amateurism.

To follow up: S2 M great rebound zone, massive presence of buyers. Monitoring for the next few days

You will notice that I do not specify what I gained or lost per trade. This does not matter, what is noted is adherence to money management and its internal rules for opening a position.

A losing trade that had to be taken can have a good score because, statistically, it had to be taken. A winning trade can get a bad score because we were just lucky. We note the technical skill, the quality of the trade and adherence to our trading rules. We are looking for discipline which is the key to regularity in trading. The financial result is of no importance in this process. It is only the consequence.

At the end of the week, in a calm atmosphere, I reread my trading journal. This enables me to visualize it, to notice that every Monday morning systematically, I take a trade through impatience at the opening because I can't wait to be on the market. Then it's up to me to find a way to contain this Monday morning impulse.

In this way you can create some very high quality material to help you progress psychologically as well as giving you technical research pointers about your trading.

There is no point in thinking that you'll remember everything, you forget 95% of your weekly trades and the conditions under which they were taken. Two weeks later, you won't remember anything, you'll have been caught up in day to day life again.

I always recommend that novices open a trading journal on the Andlil website or another forum. This forces them to analyse their day and more experienced traders can help them, point out misuse of leverage, etc. in short, it means that they can take a critical and considered look at their trading.

As we have all made the same mistakes and had the same failures, I believe this can save novice traders several years. Experienced traders pointing out where they can see issues in a novice trader's journal is a very effective and unusual service to come across.

By using a trading journal, more experienced traders can analyse their activities and identify gaps in a novice trader's behaviour. Keeping a trading journal is therefore not only a training tool for the person who keeps it, but also a reference for traders who want to help.

You really have to look at it like doing your homework after school, it's a prerequisite for progress. Take time to analyse your actions, try to understand why you took a certain poor trade, what are the trigger mechanisms that you need to build a firewall against so that you avoid repeating this type of error too often.

Loss is normal in trading, but losing without doing the necessary work to stop repeating this error is unforgivable.

Without this thinking process, taking a step back, we will always be just a blinkered trader who does not make enough effort to progress. That's the most difficult thing about trading, having enough insight to analyse what's wrong.

And in the vast majority of cases, the same reasons come up again and again. They are our personal demons, they are our own, only we can school them, reduce them or at least minimize their impact on our financial markets results. This is work that only we can do.

A trading journal is very revealing. Keeping a trading journal every day is, therefore, a matter of discipline. Discipline is the key to success in trading because you must never relax. As soon as you relax, as soon as you make a deviation from your money management, it's the end of the road.

The Andlil blog has been my trading journal for many years and sometimes I still read what I wrote and look at how I was trading four or five years ago. I can see the progress made, the hesitations, the questions, see the points where I have progressed and those where I have not yet improved, etc. it is a kind of memoir of my trading that lets me take a step back.

Trading is a daily, routine activity, there is a great risk of becoming trapped in your own habits, of no longer asking questions, of no longer evolving. However, we know that a trader who does not evolve is condemned by the implacable law of financial market Darwinism.

When trading is more regular, a trading journal is like a constant reminder of the trader's fragility, of the fact that he must always be wary of the market and especially of himself.

I noticed that when I started to neglect my trading journal, my results deteriorated, I became a little less conscientious. It is also a valuable ally in phases of doubt, where we can see how far we have come.

As an example, and to show you that even after decades of experience in the financial markets a trading journal is very useful, here is an article I wrote on 6th December 2017.

The importance of nutrition on trading

Today I have done about fifty trades on the Dax 30, and my results are strongly linked to my diet.
Trading is a sport

Trading is a high-performance sport like any other. I'm having a hard time getting this into my head. But to achieve optimal results in trading, you have to live like a high-performance sportsman. Sleep should not be neglected and neither should food. Here are my results for the day, about fifty trades and a very difficult start to the day.

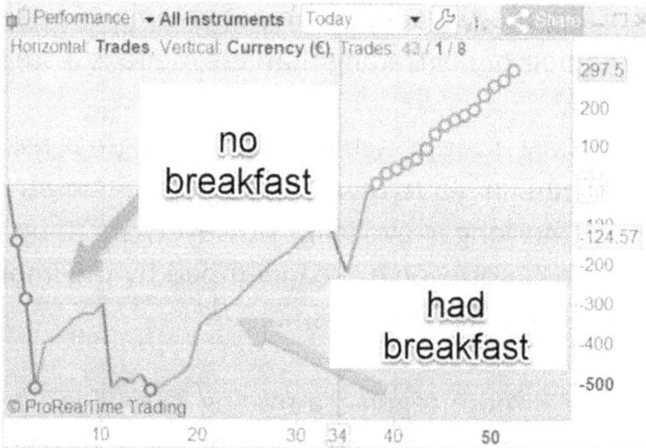

As is too often the case, I started my day without breakfast. The penalty was immediate, relentless, my first trades all went into the red.

I didn't give myself the best odds to succeed. The consequence was that I had to slog all morning to make up for the loss I made in the first few minutes. Can you imagine a sportsman starting a competition on an empty stomach? No, of course not.

And yet, while trading is the most demanding activity I have ever been able to do, I neglected that. I have tried to verify this over time. And I found a strong correlation between the absence of breakfast and the success rate of the first 10 trades of the day.

Trading on an empty stomach does not seem to be good. The brain runs more slowly, we don't have enough carbohydrates to feed it. I feel more nervous or aggressive, certainly less patient. With a full stomach, I'm less frustrated. I feel as satisfied as a newly fed baby. Probably a remnant of childhood.

But this has an influence on my trading that appears to be significant. So I will adapt and force myself to have breakfast in the morning.

Nourishment in trading

Therefore, I am going to think about having a balanced diet which is especially adapted to a trading day. Not being a dietician, I am open to all of your advice for making breakfast, lunch and dinner with this in mind. I plan to trade from 8am to

10pm non-stop, starting from 2018. Therefore, I must not neglect anything and especially not my diet. My mind must stay quick and alert. Feel free to tell me about your typical breakfasts and other meals. This way, I can summarise them to inspire as many people as possible. Nothing should be neglected in trading. Even less so the trading machine that is our body and our neurons (valid for both elective and automatic trading)."

Thanks to my trading journal I was able to relate bad starts in my trading days to my diet. Since then I have had breakfast every morning and my trading has become more regular.

Give yourself this quality of reflection and analysis by starting a trading journal. If you trade without a trading journal, you forget a lot of the experience you gained during the day on the markets. And imagine the wealth of information that this will reveal for you in six months, one year, two years, three years, etc. A real gold mine to improve your trading.

Therefore, if you would like, and after you have introduced yourself, I invite you to open your trading journal on the Andlil.com Forum. In this way you can get a perspective and possibly some friendly advice about what you are doing.

This is the first step in your progress, doing some Paper Trading and keeping a trading journal that will serve you all your trading life in your quest for perfection.

5

TRADING, THE QUEST FOR PERFECTION

Now that I have stressed the importance of Paper Trading for beginners and the fundamental role that your trading journal can play throughout your trading career, I would like to share my perspective on trading.

Trading does not tolerate approximation, there is no room for error. Everyone makes money with trading at some point. Making money on a regular basis, that is the real challenge. And to achieve this, to obtain the peace of mind that comes with regular trading gains, there is only one way: the quest for perfection.

The first thing I tell people I am coaching, who want to learn how to trade, or to traders, who after years of failure decide to review their trading from A to Z and even to professional traders who want to optimize their results, is that trading is above all a quest for perfection.

Whatever your level, beginner, experienced or expert, it is the cornerstone, the only obsession that the trader must have: the quest for perfection.

Everything must be thought of and thought out. There is no room for amateurism if you want tangible and sustainable trading results.

From the power of the computer you use for trading, to your choice of broker, to your command of the order placement interface, to the quality of your price data feeds, to the reinforcement of your psychological strength and resistance to stress, to your sleep quality, to work on your trading journal, etc. everything comes into play and everything has its importance in your final result.

If you want to make money, regularly and comfortably (without stress or taking excessive risks) you must take each element in the trading chain, point by point, and optimize it.

You can be the best trader in the world and have the best money management in the world, but if your morale, the quality of your data feeds, your PC or your order placement interface are poor, your results are going to be poor. Only when each link in the chain is solid can your trading become qualitative. Material and technical elements will no longer disrupt or interfere with your progress.

Your broker will be reliable, your equipment will be optimized and run smoothly, and your psychology will be strengthened.

You will finally be able to concentrate on the essential, on the very essence of trading, flawless actions repeated 10 times, 100 times, 1,000 times, 10,000 times.

Now let's concern ourselves with finding a reliable broker, an efficient trading interface and optimized computer equipment so that all the material problems do not interfere with our thinking, which must be focused solely on perfecting the actions required for our next trade.

6

WHICH BROKER TO CHOOSE?

The choice of your trading broker is as important as your choice of equipment. Your broker is your partner to successful trading. He must be reliable and trustworthy, offering good prices and a very high quality service.

There are hundreds of brokers who are reliable to greater or lesser degrees and repeated scandals of Cypriot brokers have generally tarnished the image of brokers.

Indeed, for a lot of people, a broker is a broker. However, this is not at all the case, the difference between the world's top 5 brokers, who are highly regarded by professional traders, and brokers based on exotic islands with no regulations is like night and day. No one would dare compare a 3-star Michelin restaurant with Mr Chippie in his van, on a B road crossroads, hiding from the health services.

Worse than that, I once said that some ‘brokers’ were on a blacklist, but that didn't stop people from using them, attracted by a fictitious ‘bonus’, and then losing everything. Just because you use the name ‘chef’ or ‘broker’ does not mean that you are one.

Sending money to a foreign broker without verification is like writing a cheque to the first unknown person you meet on the street who says "I'll pay you back".

So how do you choose a reliable and trustworthy broker?

I'll show you how to spot fake brokers. Firstly, avoid getting ripped off.

Any "broker" offering you a "bonus" should be avoided. For example, you deposit £10,000 and are credited with an additional £2,000. This is simply illegal, it does not comply with the law and it is a very common type of scam.

Another well-known scam is a broker who tells you that he has an exceptional trader who will trade for you. He will, of course, promise you high and guaranteed returns. Don't laugh, many people have fallen for this, their greed makes them lose all sense.

Of course, this trader has fabulous results, he makes 50% in 15 days, and the person is then actively solicited to transfer more money so as to take advantage of this rare opportunity. The more money the person sends, the more the fake trader makes in his successful trades.

Until the day the poor dreamer asks for his money back. That "nice" trader no longer answers his phone, it becomes impossible to contact the company that is located goodness knows where. It's a little late to worry about that. Let's just remember that guaranteeing a high return is illegal and that a broker will never trade using your money, this is the epitome of a scam.

Likewise, if a broker contacts you by phone, this is illegal, you should hang up.

Warning signs

Avoid exotic brokers on far-flung islands. Simply doing this will ensure that you will avoid the worst of them. Some are not even regulated (i.e. they are not allowed to be brokers, they come and go quickly).

Think about the future. If your broker is in Australia or Bulgaria, what are you going to do if there is a problem? Your local authorities are not going to be able to do anything for you. Are you going to fly over there, look for a lawyer in situ in a language you don't speak well and with laws that you don't know anything about?

Check your broker's financial health by asking him for his quarterly balance sheets. Reliable brokers make them available to their clients on their website. Do not put your trust in a broker who refuses to show you his results.

Of course, your assets must be segregated from your broker's. They should be in a bank independent of your broker so that he has no access to them and, therefore, cannot use your money for his own purposes.

Be careful, in the European Union, if you use a bank which goes bankrupt, the bank can use your assets to bail itself out. These laws were passed after the various crises of 2008 and 2011 and are not well known.

In simple terms, you stand united with your bank in the event of bankruptcy, you are generous enough to leave all your savings to your bank so that it can repay its debts. I commend this altruism, but if you don't want to be so closely linked to your bank, you have to choose a broker for trading and not a bank.

Remember that if brokers are in Cyprus, it is not due to the good weather, it is because it is very easy to obtain a broker's licence with much more "flexible" rules than in France or Germany, etc.

As each broker has his own qualities and characteristics, and each trader has his own requirements, I can't recommend one broker over another. One broker might be excellent for equity trading, but dreadful for Forex and vice versa.

Personally, I am with ProRealTime Trading using the ProRealTime trading interface included in their Premium version.

I tested a lot of brokers before choosing the best one for me and I encourage you to do the same. You have the time, you are just starting out, choose the best broker for yourself.

For example, you could open several accounts and test their trading interfaces. You will notice that there are striking differences in speed and efficiency between brokers.

Quality of data feed

Personally, as a scalper, I need a very fast scalping interface and data feeds in ticks so that I see every trade that goes through the order book on my charts.

You should note that data feeds cost brokers a lot and many of them save money by providing truncated data feeds. Using a truncated data feed the broker sends 4 data points per 1 second, whatever the market, whereas with a normal data feed you would receive 12, 40, 80, etc. depending on volatility.

I scalp in ticks so that I can feel the market breathing and this liveliness. If I streamed a data feed, all my charts would be wrong and my results corrupted. For example, a lot of brokers offer to sell you incomplete data feeds. It's impossible to scalp with these data feeds. Scalpers are forced to switch to good old Japanese candlesticks set in minutes, which only show us elapsed time. Scalpers do not trade based on time but based on volatility that only tick candlesticks can show.

That's why I use ProRealTime Trading for trading futures. They provide me with Premium tick-by-tick data feeds, which are free if you trade a little every month, and a trading interface worthy of the name, considered one of the best for several years.

Shall we recap? A good trader needs a good broker who provides him with quality service (tick data feed) and who is reliable and controlled by effective regulatory institutions.

Now that you have found a trusted broker who gives you quality information for decision making, let's look at how we equip ourselves to make money in the financial markets: our trading station.

7

HOW TO CHOOSE A TRADING STATION

Your choice of trading equipment is as important as your choice of broker. You need equipment adapted to your type of trading that you are comfortable with and that is quick and secure to place your trades.

You might have a solid trading method and fool proof money management but if your trading station becomes sluggish at the first peak of high volatility, you could lose your year's gains.

Some people think that having good computer equipment is not very important. They are usually the first to complain when they can no longer place orders in times of crisis. Effectively, their PC and/or internet connection can no longer manage the data inflow. In the middle of a volatility crisis, their computer freezes and they are in a total panic and can't leave the market.

Whilst a trader with decent, optimized equipment can calmly take advantage of the situation with no stress. Remember, trading does not tolerate approximation, every link in the chain must be sound. A single weak link could be a disaster in the true sense of the word.

Imagine that you are making a leveraged purchase and the market collapses without you being able to react. Every second that passes will feel like an eternity if you are a trader on your own account. It could totally jeopardize the success of your business or cost you years of savings.

As hardware evolves very quickly, there will be frequent updates on this topic in the private area of the site. Including, useful components for setting up your trading station, trading stations and laptops that I feel are a good compromise between quality and price and on software to optimize it all.

So I will be very concise and general in this book.

There is no ideal trading station because each trader is different and does not have the same needs. A trader on his own account, trading 8 hours to 12 hours a day favours a high-performance, silent trading station with quality equipment that will last for several years. A trader who trades in the evening on his way home from work is usually satisfied with the family computer or a laptop.

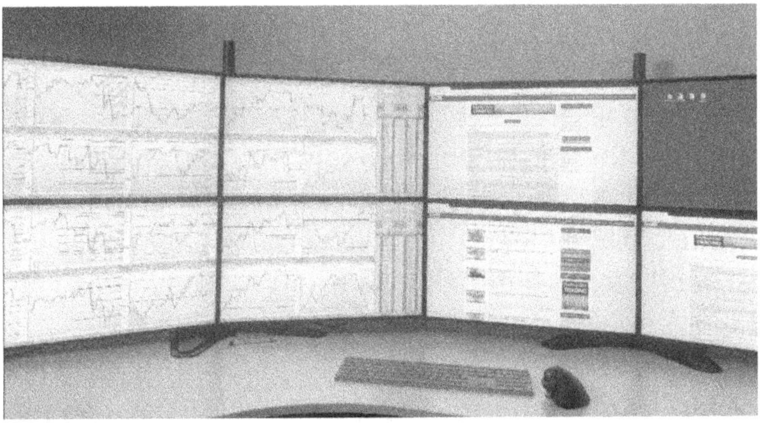

My 8-screen trading station

But we can list the essential elements to have a versatile, durable and efficient trading station.

Choice of microprocessor: your PC's brain must be powerful. I prefer i7 microprocessors which are extremely powerful and offer an unrivalled price/performance ratio. i3 microprocessors would have trouble managing volatility peaks if you have too many charts open, i5 microprocessors are powerful enough, but if you can spend a few more pounds, I strongly recommend the i7 versions.

RAM, your computer's memory: with modern operating systems, you need at least 8 GB which will just do, ideally go for 16 GB, which is the best compromise. If you have a few more pounds to spend, go straight for 32 GB, this should last you a few years without having to upgrade.

The **motherboard:** this is the air traffic controller for all your components. Nowadays there aren't any bad motherboards, you don't need to buy high-end motherboards, and they are essentially made for geeks who want to optimize their system by increasing microprocessor frequency, for example. With a trading station, we are, above all, looking for configuration stability.

The hard disk: there is no possible compromise, an SSD hard disk enables you to significantly boost your computer. If your PC is slow and old, an SSD could give your PC a boost. Having tested several brands, I find that Samsung, whatever the version, stands out well above the crowd.

The graphics card for multiscreen: to be clear, it's with the graphics card that trading station sellers are going to rip you off. In their configurations, they have the most up to date video cards, perfect for 3D, video editing, etc. but for a trading station, displaying figures and some charts, low-end, mid-range cards are more than enough.

For HD screens there are some excellent graphics cards, capable of managing 2 to 3 screens with no difficulty. How much? £50. Of course, you won't play the latest popular video games with this card, but it will display about twenty charts with no problem. My graphics card that lets me display four, 4k screens cost as little as £250. So avoid graphic cards costing £800 to £1000, you're being ripped off.

Power supply: this element is often forgotten in configurations, but it is important for your system's stability and life expectancy. Favour Gold or Platinum power supplies, the extra cost is really worth it.

The box and fans: I am really obsessive about these elements. As I am next to my PC for between 10 and 14 hours a day, I want it to be as quiet as possible. To achieve this, there are padded housings that suppress noise. I particularly like the Silencio range from Cooler Master and Noctua fans, but I am not a specialist in this field, I have only tested 3 manufacturers.

The screen: opt for a quality screen with flicker reduction and blue light technologies. Your eyes are your working tool and you are going to spend thousands of hours peering at your charts. I recommend that you have two to four screens to trade with the utmost comfort. More than comfort, this will also give you a broader view of the market with more charts. This increases both your comfort level and your effectiveness.

Mouse and trackball: often overlooked, a mouse is important in your trading for two reasons:
1) You need a fast mouse to transmit the information. Between a high-end mouse and a low-end mouse, you can gain more than 50 ms. Some people battle with their ADSL connection to get the ping down from 30 ms to 15 ms, but they overlook their mouse.
2) With the time you spend using your mouse, you may experience pain in your hands after a while. You can prevent this by using an ergonomic mouse or trackball. When I am writing, I much prefer the Logitech MX Ergo (which is highly efficient in reducing muscle tension).

The box: I strongly recommend silent boxes that dampen all the vibrations and various noises that can come from your PC. This reduces fatigue and increases concentration. If your PC vibrates or whistles, whilst you are trading for 10 hours straight, it affects you. Even if you are no longer conscious of the noise, your brain registers it.

Cabling: generally a totally neglected part of a trading station's optimization. It is absolutely crucial to use category seven or eight cables to connect your trading station to your internet box.

The basic cables, provided by your internet service provider, are disastrous. They are generally category five and the quality is deplorable. For a few pounds, you can change all the wiring and increase safety, efficiency and speed. Just changing a cable between the PC and the box saved me a few milliseconds and cost less than five pounds.

In the private area of the website, there is a selection of articles on each of the components making up your computer, from the microprocessor to the RJ45 cables, based on budget and the item's effectiveness.

Being a geek, this part will be updated very regularly with material that I test myself. Effectively, if you bought this book in 2020, this chapter is totally obsolete, but the information on your private area of the Andlil.com website is up to date.
Also, think about getting a good chair that looks after your back, you are going to sit on it for a good few hours.

Laptop or desktop computer for trading?

For professional use, there is no question about it, a desktop computer is the best option. An intensively used laptop has a maximum life expectancy of two to three years. A desktop PC's life expectancy is much longer and problematic parts can be changed without having to buy a complete configuration.

With a laptop, apart from changing the hard disk and increasing RAM, it isn't possible to upgrade it. Additionally, and this is the most important point for a trading station, microprocessors and RAM in laptops are much less powerful. This poses problems when volatility peaks, the computer freezes, prices are no longer updated quickly, etc. The quality of your internet connection is, of course, essential, but a laptop or a low-powered desktop computer will quickly become saturated and give you problems.

I have bought the latest and most powerful laptops, from MacBook Pro to Alienware. Upgraded them to the maximum with an i7, 32 GB of RAM, SSD etc. Nothing makes any difference. Laptop computers, to date, do not yet have enough power to handle a Fed or FOMC announcement.
And now that you have a trading station worthy of the name, here are some tips to maintain it and keep it at optimum performance.

8

OPTIMIZE AND SECURE YOUR TRADING STATION

Secure your trading station

As part of your trading station's internet security, I strongly recommend that you buy APC inverters which cost about thirty pounds. If there is a power failure, which will happen to you sooner or later, the inverters take over for a few minutes. This gives you enough time to close your position without having to panic. Of course, to be effective, you have to attach one APC to your computer and another to your internet box. This way, if there is a power failure, your internet connection will still work as well as your PC.

Anecdote
A few years ago I lived in a house in a rural area. I was trading Nikkei 225 futures. It was three in the morning. I was in the process of buying 10 lots. There was a power failure in the middle of the trading session. I couldn't close my position on my mobile phone, my network's coverage was abysmal. So there I was, at three in the morning, in my pyjamas. In my panic, I knocked up the neighbours to see if they had any electricity. The result of that sad night was a loss of €5,000. The electricity came back on quarter of an hour later when the market had dropped. Imagine that, whilst I could do nothing, the market was collapsing! Since then, I have had inverters.

For security, I trade with my main PC and I always have a backup PC right next to me, in case my main PC fails. I knew a trader who lost a lot of money because he was trading on his desktop PC, using a screen. And his screen broke down. The silliest of things to happen.

I have, of course, heard of internet connection backups. I always have my mobile phone to hand and charged, so that I can place an order on my Smartphone in case there is any problem.

If you are in a relationship, the best thing is for you each to have your own mobile phone subscription with different telephone operators. If one of the telephone operator services fails, it is likely that the second will still work. I have already done this when trading on the move.

By the way, it is worth noting that a Wi-Fi connection should be avoided, it is not as fast or as stable as shielded RJ45 cables. Your neighbour switches on the microwave, your child closes a door and this affects the transmission of your orders. You can run several dozen meters of RJ45 cable along your skirting boards to connect your PC to your box with no problems, and it will still look as good. I have 25 meters of RJ45 cable running along my skirting board and door frames. If I can do it, with my DIY skills, an eight-year-old child can do it, and probably better than me. Do it!

Software optimization

If you trade using an Apple computer, there is some good news, you don't have to do anything.

If you trade using a computer equipped with Windows, here is some software that you can install to maintain your PC's speed (or it will give it a boost if you have never done it before)

These software programs make it very easy to maintain, repair, secure and optimize your PC. The free versions are adequate, they still do an excellent job. If you are a real perfectionist and lazy, like me, the paid versions enable automation of these tasks.

At the time of writing, I recommend two free and effective software programs.

Ccleaner
https://www.ccleaner.com

Advanced SystemCare
https://www.iobit.com/advancedsystemcarefree.php

There are also updates for these optimization tips and software recommendations in the private area of the website. One tip that could be very useful: if you trade using your broker's web interface, install as many browsers as possible (Internet Explorer, Opera, Firefox, Safari, Chrome, etc.) and test their speeds. Performance gaps can be very impressive, especially if you use a laptop or a low-end PC. You will be very surprised to see the differences in speed from one internet browser to another.

Install all these browsers on your computer and test them. The differences in speed depend on the components of your PC, its status and the broker's web trading interface collectively. Therefore, I can't recommend one more exclusively than another. The results will vary depending on your broker, the power of your computer, etc.

I will conclude this chapter by talking about antivirus software.

Basically, for security and efficiency, you should ideally dedicate your trading station to trading only. So don't install video games, don't surf download sites, etc. If you trade on a family PC, keep your antivirus software up to date. If your computer is dedicated to trading only and you know the basic security rules (don't surf suspicious websites, don't open emails with attachments, etc.), you can disable the antivirus program, because computers running Windows 10 already have an effective antivirus program called Windows Defender.

In 99% of cases, it is effective and, if you are conscientious, in 100% of cases. Personally, I have been using PCs on a daily basis for 30 years and I have never had any viruses, malware, etc. on my PCs. I am satisfied with Windows' basic protection. But I must emphasize, I am extremely conscientious about using my PCs.

Why am I telling you this? Some antivirus software will slow down your data flows from the financial markets. They analyse each tick that comes in before authorizing it. It takes time, it takes up your PC's resources, it slows down reception and transmission of orders, etc.

Additionally, I know from experience that many people have two antivirus programs at the same time: Windows Defender and another one that they have bought. So they end up with two antivirus programs each analysing the data feed in turn. If you don't have a really powerful PC when there is high volatility that can cause problems.

To summarize
Trade using a high-performance computer which can deal with the effects of volatility, carry out regular updates, maintain and optimize your computer using appropriate software, connect it to the internet box with a quality RJ 45 cable, use 2 inverters to ensure security in case of a power failure, as a precaution, always have a small PC or tablet and a secondary internet connection (via a Smartphone for example) in case of emergency.

Well, there you have it, less to worry about, no anxiety about trading, everything is secure, everything is under control, you can't do better, all that is left to do is trade.

But what should you trade? There is a vast choice.

9

WHY TRADE INDICES?

I am often asked why I mainly trade indices when I could also invest in equities, Forex, cryptocurrencies, etc.

Personally, I quickly found that indices were what suited me best for trading and that's where I get my best results. Additionally, I find them much easier and more simple to trade.

Of course, you need to determine which type of instrument you are most comfortable with when you are training with Paper Trading.

Be curious, you may be an excellent trader on the Belgian BEL 20 index or on Futures trading in orange juice or Apple shares.

The time you spend Paper Trading gives you the luxury of being curious and discovering a range of different instruments.

In a world where people are becoming more and more paranoid, I am always surprised that very few novice traders start trading indices. It is true that brokers do not highlight indices in their messages because that's where they have the lowest margins.

Remember that one of the great strengths of indices is that they can't be manipulated. Actually, you can't directly make the index change by buying or selling indices, it changes with the prices of the securities that comprise it. An index is the weighted mathematical average of the 30, 40, 100, 500 or 2,000 corporate securities at a point in time.

When we talk about the Nasdaq 100, we are talking about an index calculated on the top 100 companies in the Nasdaq. When we talk about the CAC 40, that index is calculated with the prices of the top 40 French companies. For the Japanese Nikkei 225 index, I'll let you guess.

To manipulate an index, the financial cost would be infinitely higher than the expected benefits and you would be instantly identified.

In fact, in theory, you would have to buy or sell tens of thousands of company shares simultaneously, including all the shares that make up the index, to vary an index by only a few points. This would also result in 150 years in federal prison in the United States of America (with a reduced sentence), for price manipulation. So a sensible person would never spend and risk hundreds of millions of dollars to vary an index by a few points.

Note
This also puts an end to a stubborn urban legend, that of brokers trying to trigger a stop. Do you really think that a broker would spend £50,000,000,000, buying shares on a massive scale, to try to hit the stop signal for a customer with a £1 micro-lot? The great strength of indices is that no one has the financial capacity to manipulate them. Moreover, the price of the indices is global, it is the same for all traders. On the other hand, Forex does not have centralized quotations, all brokers offer their own price, and cryptocurrencies have such low volumes that with a few million euros you could do what you want with them. And these are often the products that novice traders look for.

In some ways, you could say that, with an index, Money management is already integrated because it is simply a basket of shares. You don't put all your eggs in one basket. If you buy Nasdaq 100, you are automatically diversifying into a hundred or so American high-tech companies. By buying the CAC 40 index, you are putting emphasis on the petrochemical industries. With the Footsie, you are favouring financial companies. When trading the Dax 30, the weight of
Industry is higher than many other indices.

This is very interesting because your index cannot go bankrupt, unlike a publicly-traded company. If the company goes bankrupt, you lose your entire investment. If a Dax 30 company goes bankrupt, it is automatically replaced by the 31st German company. The effect of this bankruptcy on the index is therefore considerably limited. That's why there is risk mitigation by trading indices as opposed to shares.

Risk is the death of the trader. You really have to get that into your head if you want to have a chance in trading, you have to avoid risk. Risk is lucrative once, twice, three times and the fourth time it takes you down. It is your main enemy with yourself in trading.

Trading shares is riskier than holding an index, because the company's historical CEO may have a health problem, the company may be sued, it may recall a defective product, it may lose a lawsuit, be denied access to a market by authorities, etc. and all of these have major consequences. Every day there are some shares that increase or drop by 10%, 25%, etc. An index that loses or gains 10% is a historical event. It is still talked about 20 years later.

Stock market novices get excited by these large fluctuations because they imagine, of course, that they will make 25%. They can also take a 25% slap in the face and take years to recover, all the more if they have low capital. But they avoid thinking about this. This feeling of omnipotence is very dangerous on the financial markets: "it won't happen to me."

The bad news is that the market has absolutely no awareness of our existence, so there is no justice or injustice in stock price fluctuations. They vary as they must, whether we are there or not. Never forget that we are zooplankton on the stock market. If we forget, the financial markets will remind us of our insignificance very quickly. You, therefore, have to trade with great humility. A trader with a big ego has a rather short life expectancy.

As you don't put all your eggs in one basket (like you do when buying cryptocurrency, a share or trading in Forex), you benefit from the dynamism of the global world economy because you invest in 30, 50, 100 companies. If one of these companies is in trouble, that doesn't stop the index from rising.

Similarly, with indices, you smooth out the risk. You benefit from the positive or negative dynamics, depending on whether you buy or sell the index, of the global economy. With a little experience, you can see the medium to long-term trend on indices. So if you don't have an aggressive short-term strategy, you can let yourself get carried away.

Each index has its own personality and that's what I like best about indices, they all have a character. Each index has a different rhythm that adapts, to a greater or lesser extent, to scalping, day trading or swing trading. They are like human beings, they are typified, and they have their own character traits. And you can inevitably find an index that matches your personality as a trader.

Of course, in the same manner that you do not behave in the same way with an aggressive or passive person, you must have techniques specific to each index. Of course, I do not trade the Dax 30, Nasdaq 100 or Dow Jones 30 in scalping in exactly the same way.

This may come as a surprise, but trading indices is ethical. You can explain it to your friends who judge traders without having even the slightest knowledge of economics. By buying or selling indices, you have absolutely no impact on the share price, and therefore on the lives of employees, and all the other blabla we hear from the media. You have no impact on the countries' debt, you have no impact on raw materials, etc. You buy and sell an index. Directly investing in an index does not change stock prices. You have an absolutely neutral ecological footprint.

On the other hand, if your friends have life insurance, they have an impact on the economic life and the lives of "people". For example, they speculate on the debt of countries. Generally, they will not appreciate you explaining this to them, but you have to get them out of their economic obscurantism.

In conclusion, indices trading is a secure form of trading with integrated money management. The risks of index trading are lower than on other products because an index cannot go bankrupt.

There is, therefore, great subtlety in trading indices. You have to know them, each one has its personality, its rhythm and, over time, you will learn to master them.

You will get up in the morning and just by looking at the first trades you will know if your index is in a bad mood, in a good mood, if it is hesitant, if it is afraid, if it is euphoric, etc. You may end up deciphering your favourite index's mood better than you do your partner's when you get out of bed.

10

UNDERSTANDING FUTURES

There is often some confusion with index futures among novice traders who do not understand why these futures are not the same price as the cash index, which is the benchmark index. We often see on financial market forums conspiracy theories or the idea that there is speculation and the major players anticipate a decrease or increase in the index in the coming months. This has absolutely nothing to do with either conspiracy theory or excessive speculation.

How is an index calculated on a future?

An Index Future is not the same price as the cash index, the difference is mainly explained by interest rates applied at maturity and scheduled dividend detachments during its maturity. (Where an Index Future takes into account the ex-divident value.)

An index future price, therefore, varies according to the cash price, interest rates and any scheduled dividend detachments. It is all very simple.

It is important to remember that the cash index is not traded directly, it is a mathematical calculation of the weighted price of the shares it comprises. It is important to know the index's weighting, each index has a more or less heavy weighting in a particular economic sector.

Therefore, on the CAC 40, Oil and Chemicals are significant, the weight of financials on the FTSE 100 is overwhelming, the Dax 30 is a more "industrial" index etc.

Futures operate on maturities

Each index future has its own maturities. The CAC 40 futures have monthly maturities, while the Dax 30 and the American Index Futures have quarterly maturities (March, June, September and December) that always end on the 3rd Friday of each month at a different time (e.g. 13:00 for the Dax 30, 16:00 for the CAC 40 Index Future).

When switching from one maturity to another, for example from March to June, there is what is called a rollover (which can be automatic or manual). Investors close their positions in the index before maturity to reposition themselves for the next maturity. If they don't, their money is "blocked" until the end of the month (delivery), so everyone does it unless they are careless. It is also an opportunity to end a month or quarter and perhaps initiate different positions.

This is why there can be "surprise" candlesticks or a lot of lively movements a few minutes before the deadline if a large index is "stuck" for any reason (sometimes this is the final blow before a Hedge Fund's bankruptcy. They hope for a miracle up to the last moment, or they try to maximize their earnings over a specific maturity (when there is a quarterly bonus for example)).

Futures are linked to rates

An Index Future may, therefore, be worth more or less than the benchmark cash index due to interest rates (negative or positive) and scheduled dividend detachments. All futures are therefore impacted by interest rates (which can change daily).

Of course, interest rates are not the same on all Futures and depend on whether your index is European, American, Japanese, etc. They depend on central banks' monetary policy. Some central banks may decide to attract capital, as the Australian central bank was able to do for a few years. Under certain conditions, it was possible to receive money every night by selling the Australian index, for example.

Futures can be impacted by dividends

Since Index Futures follow the cash price, they are of course affected by dividend detachments, which impact the price of certain indices. Whether or not the index reflects the ex-dividend effect in its price depends entirely on the cash index. The CAC 40 future is impacted by dividend detachments, but not the Dax 30 for example.

Understandably, on the last day of maturity, the price of futures is equal to the price of cash because there are no further possible effects from future interest rates or ex-dividend dates. So, the closer we get to the Index Future's maturity date, the closer its price "sticks" to the cash index. There is, therefore, no conspiracy theory or excessive speculation when the price of a future differs from the price of the bench-mark cash index.

Everything makes sense. So, there is no conspiracy when you see a significant gap between the price of the cash index and the price of the future. It is simply that the interest rates and dividends that fall due before maturity are included.

Similarly, this says absolutely nothing about the trend expected in the coming weeks.

How many young novice traders have lost money thinking that?

Futures operate with an order book

With Futures, there is no guarantee of liquidity, or that you can enter or exit the market at the asking price. You place your order in the order book and it's first come first served.

Sometimes the price is reached, but your order is not executed. For example, I place an order to sell 2 YM lots (Dow Jones 30 Futures) at 26006 in the order book. There are already 10 visible batches, the number then increases to 12.

(I specify 10 visible batches because there are iceberg orders, i.e. those that do not appear visually in the order book. They are hidden. Anyone can use iceberg orders. There might actually be 50 lots, but I have no way of knowing).

If the price rises and buyers hit on level 26006, if there are 12 lots being bought, my order will be executed. But if only 9 lots are hit at this price and the price goes down, then there will be 3 lots left for sale and my orders will not be executed as they are at positions 11 and 12 in the queue and there is one person before me (position 10).

If 11 batches are hit, I will then have 1 partial order executed: 1 of my lots will be sold and the second lot will still be waiting for a potential buyer.

That is a summary of how the order book works to give you an idea. There is no point in spending a lot of time describing the subtleties of the order book, you will find out about it using your demo account.

Now let's look at leverage, the novice trader's worst enemy which can also become a good friend for more experienced traders.

11

HOW TO CALCULATE YOUR LEVERAGE

It is extremely important for new traders to understand what leverage is.

Effectively, they have to calculate it when developing their Money management, understand its effects and the risks they take if they have too much leverage.

Futures offer the use of leverage. It is around 10, at most, on Futures indices where margins are applied at the end of the trading day.

If you have €10,000 in your trading account and are offered leverage of 10, you can buy up to €100,000 worth of financial products.

Practically, this means that if you take leverage of 10 on an index, your gains and losses could be:

With a 1% change in the index in your favour: your capital increases by 10%
With a 1% adverse change in the index: your capital will lose 10%

With a leverage of 4 (much more reasonable):
+1% in your favour gives +4% on your portfolio, -1% to your disadvantage gives -4% on your portfolio's valuation.

You need to seriously consider the devastating results that too high a leverage might have.

With traditional securities, **leverage** is normally 5, and for novices, traditional brokers authorise leverage of between 2 and 3 at most. Staying within these leverage limits is safer and more sensible. **Above all, a** trader must last over time rather than flash and burn.

It is therefore important, vital even, to know how to calculate your leverage when trading Futures.

How to calculate leverage

You must take three things into account: the instrument that you use, its price and the capital that you have available.

Example: using **Dow Jones 30** Futures at 1$ a point.

The price of the Dow Jones is 25,000 points. When you buy a batch of Dow Jones (YM) at $1 per point, you buy at 25,000 * 1 = $25,000. You need to know how much you have on your account.

If you are trading with $10,000, you are already leveraged at 2.5 (25,000/10,000 = 2.5).

If you are trading with $25,000, you are leveraged at 1 (25,000/25,000 = 1).

If you are trading with $50,000, you are leveraged at 0.5 (25,000/50,000 = 0.5).

In summary, you need to multiply the point value (€1, €5, €25, etc.) by the price of the instrument that you are trading to know how much you are really investing. Then you divide this figure by your capital.

Knowing what your leverage is on your positions is the basis of **Money management**.

When starting out, ideally, you should use as little leverage as possible, or even be under-leveraged to significantly reduce your stress level when trading. However, we will see that it is possible to trade with leverage without any risk during aggressive pyramid trading with guaranteed stops.

To be an effective trader, you need to understand the economic environment, central bank policies, investment flows, etc. The trading world is also a great way to learn how the world works.

For example, an oil trader must have a good knowledge of geopolitics. A trader on the Nasdaq 100 must be interested in the latest news from GAFAM companies (Google, Apple, Facebook, Amazon and Microsoft).

You also need to understand the global economic environment. I am going to sum up the minimum that you'll need to survive on the stock market in the next chapter.

12

ECONOMIC CONCEPTS AND THE PACE OF FINANCIAL MARKETS

It is impossible, in just a few lines, to give a novice trader a proper economic culture. This is acquired over time, through reflection and experience.

However, I can give you some great ideas that you should always keep in mind when trading.

Perhaps the most important thing: America is Number One

The United States of America sets the pace on the financial markets. If the American financial markets goes up, it has magnetic power over all the other indices. If the New York market falls sharply, the whole world follows, indexes in Europe, Asia, etc.

Because of its economic power, its financial strength (60% of the CAC 40 is held directly or indirectly by Americans via hedge funds, pension funds, etc.), the weight of its companies in the internet field, Google, Apple, Facebook, Amazon and Microsoft (GAFAM) and its consumption (more than 20% of world consumption comes from Americans), we cannot trade without taking an interest in the American economy.

The United States is more than a country, it is the engine of the global economy. When Hollywood releases a film or a television series, it's for 7 billion people's immediate viewing. France did not have the same ambitions with its national hit TV series. When we produce in France, we usually think local (national) and if all goes well, as a second step, maybe move on to a European level in a few countries. In the United States of America their local market is the planet Earth.

American power is a stronger cultural force than any other. Everyone has eaten, eats or will eat a Big Mac, will watch a Netflix series, knows the names of American actors, singers, athletes, Mickey Mouse and Donald Duck. All little boys, whether African, European, Asian, etc. dream of being a Jedi and having a lightsaber. We use Google daily for our searches (I challenge you to name a search engine from a different country), it is a world culture.

When Bob and Barbie are in good spirits, when they buy heavily using their credit cards (via debt), factories in China run at full capacity, jobs are created in Europe (20% of private jobs in France are directly or indirectly linked to the American economy's healthy state). In short, Americans drive the global economy.

That's why for us traders the quarterly results of American companies are fundamental, they set the trend for a few weeks. Similarly, U.S. unemployment statistics are very important.

If you trade the CAC 40, the results of French unemployment or growth have NO impact on CAC 40 share prices. No one follows them except beginners who think it is logical, no one discusses them except commentators who have nothing to say or who know nothing about the financial markets.

As for the election of the President of the French Republic, it has absolutely no impact on the CAC 40. Journalists systematically try to see a correlation between the presidential election and the opening of the French stock exchange the next day, but this makes no sense. A closing at +2% or -2% of the American markets, that's what sets the trend the next day on the CAC 40.

China is the world's workshop

The next country to watch very closely when trading is China. Effectively, China is a major manufacturing and industrial power. It is therefore very important to monitor the country's industrial and manufacturing production indicators. If the Chinese economy is growing, if its order books are full, etc. it's because the global economy is doing well. Demand is high.

In a nutshell, one could say that by monitoring the American economy, we are taking the pulse of the world's morale. We still remember, on a global scale, the catastrophe that the slowdown in American consumption was during the various crises. It put tens of millions of people out of work in China and completely crushed European growth.

By monitoring the Chinese economy, we take the pulse of the consumption dynamics of the entire planet.

In practice, therefore, we must constantly monitor the economic news of these two countries, bearing in mind, however, that the weight of the United States of America is much greater in any event. That's why a good trader monitors American companies' publications every quarter, monitors American economic statistics, etc.

The overwhelming weight of central banks

Since the 2008 crisis, the weight of central banks has increased exponentially. The long-term underlying trend is determined by their monetary policy. Oversimplifying, here's how it works:

Central banks lower interest rates: this is very favorable to the financial markets. Effectively, the lower the interest rates, the more investors position themselves in the equity market, which offers better return prospects than investing their money at extremely low interest rates.

Central banks raise interest rates: this is not a good signal for the financial markets. Effectively, if an investor can safely invest his money with an acceptable rate of return, he will do so. He will even tend, if interest rates are very high, to sell his shares, which remain an uncertain investment and then deposit his money at high guaranteed rates.

This is why the decisions of central banks such as the Fed and the ECB are major events in the financial markets' year. Every comma in the central bank's statement and every intervention by the President of the ECB or the Fed is highly monitored. Investors try to detect change or continuity in monetary policy in the following months.

A major change in the direction of the financial markets, a sudden reversal, is often the result of a change in central bank policy.

The role of central banks is all the more important because they are aware, after Alan Greenspan's mistakes, of the importance of their decisions.

While the American economy was booming, the Fed President raised interest rates too quickly. Effectively, he wanted to engineer, in his words "a soft landing for the American economy" which had too strong growth and which was beginning to show inflationary pressures. Alan Greenspan, who experienced hyperinflation in Europe in the 1930s, was determined to prevent inflation from developing.

The result is that the American economy did not land smoothly, it crashed violently. By raising interest rates too quickly, he triggered the subprime crisis, which still has global repercussions 10 years later. Since that sad experience, central banks, whose main mission is to prevent inflation from spreading, have become aware of the overwhelming weight of their decisions.

To summarise
Even if you don't know anything about macroeconomics or microeconomics, you have to remember three things: The weight of the American economy is absolutely overwhelming. The results of U.S. unemployment have a much greater impact on European financial markets than national results. One saying sums it up: when the United States of America sneezes, the whole world gets a cold. China is the world's workshop. Chinese economic statistics provide a global view of the state of worldwide demand. Declining industrial and manufacturing production in China can cause all world indices to fall because it is not a good sign in terms of worldwide demand. If demand is not good, companies may make less profit. The decisions of the major central banks on their rates is a major catalyst for the long-term trend of the markets.

The rhythm of the Financial Markets

Due to the weight of American companies and the decisions of central banks, the financial markets' year is not smooth. We don't trade in the same way at different times of the year.

I suggest that you list them and memorise them well because you will have to adapt to this rhythm.

The quarterly results of American companies are very closely monitored. They take place quarterly, four times a year, of course.

This moment is surely the most eagerly awaited highlight for all traders. It is an opportunity to take stock of the state of the economy by observing the micro economy in detail.

Have companies made higher profits than expected, has real consumption increased? Have banking shares suffered?

The quarterly balance sheets of U.S. companies therefore provide a pulse on the global economy and allow us to take stock on a sector-by-sector basis. Managers make their decisions based on company projections, expected dividends, etc.

Careful, I'm talking about American companies. Only they create this anticipation. The world holds its breath when Alphabet (Google's parent company), Amazon, Microsoft, etc. publish their results. When it comes to BEL 20 companies (Belgian index), traders all over the world don't care a bit, even Belgian traders (sorry).

Between each quarterly maturity, investors rely on macroeconomic statistical data: unemployment figures, GDP trends, etc., and try to discern developments for the coming months. For the three months between two corporate balance sheet results, companies' situations are envisioned using macroeconomic data.

Companies' results are, therefore, a form of Solomon's judgement, we no longer need to imagine, we have the answers, hence the sometimes abrupt readjustments by managers. Some companies may collapse and others may take off, so it's a volatile time for equity traders.

In the same way, decisions of the (big) central banks are eagerly awaited by all traders around the world.

On the very day of the decision the markets are tense. This is almost felt physically, the order books slowly dry up, and professionals withdraw and wait. These are extremely dangerous days when beginners and experienced traders alike should not trade.

Generally speaking, we don't trade when there are announcements. We never anticipate an announcement, it's not about the financial markets any more, and it's about gambling, like at a casino. No one is psychic.

This is when you can spot the professional traders and the amateurs. The pros don't get excited, they wait calmly. Novices get excited by the smell of blood. They know there can be a lot of volatility and they imagine making a lot of money. What they don't understand is that the blood might be theirs.

When you're lucky enough to know the time a potential hurricane will hit, what do you do?

Old sailors return to port and watch the spectacle from a safe place. Young buccaneers rush to "be in it", to be there.

You need to know not to trade when situations are potentially dangerous. A trader tries to make a living by minimising risk, not chasing after it. In this case he's not a trader, he's more of a cowboy.

To complete the financial markets' rhythm, there are periods of the year when volatility is normally lower, with a few exceptions. July and August are often slow, very slow, too slow. You have to adapt to these periods and especially not give in to trading out of boredom.

Now that we know the main economic catalysts that make financial markets vary, we will look at some of the financial market paradoxes that often create misunderstanding among novice traders.

13

I DON'T UNDERSTAND ANYTHING ABOUT THE FINANCIAL MARKETS!

Many apprentice traders are sometimes desperate because they don't understand financial market logic. The numbers are good, the financial markets decline. The numbers are bad, the financial markets climb. And when they don't understand, they start clamouring about scams and manipulation, etc.

I'm going to decipher some common financial market "scams" for you. I hope you understood the irony in that statement, these are not "scams", but simply a lack of knowledge of how financial markets work or of the logic of investors. When we do not understand the mechanisms, the simplest solution is to see them as manipulation rather than looking for logic. Let's face it, even if it hurts the narcissism of a lot of traders, the market is always right. It's an immutable rule.

Financial markets are very basic and they function like a group subconscious (we will come back to this in the section on the psychology of trading).

You have two choices with financial markets: either they go up or they go down. It couldn't be simpler. They go up if there are more buyers, they go down if there are more sellers.

Our opinion on the world economic situation, the health of a company, etc. is of absolutely no importance on the financial markets unless you are trading with capital of 100 billion dollars. So the question is not 'what do we think?' But 'what do the majority of stakeholders think?' (even if we think it's daft).

So what gives us accurate and important information for our trading and the global financial market climate is not the announcement of a company's result or economic statistics, but the interpretation and reaction that occurs.

Let me give you some examples to make it clear:

A company announces an increase in profits and turnover. Strong positive signals. But the stock starts to drop significantly. Generally this leads to a total lack of understanding among apprentice traders. If the results are good, the stock price must increase, it seems logical.

The reality is more complex because investors' anticipation of the company's earnings may be lower than their expectations. Disappointed, they prefer to sell their shares to cash in their profits and invest in another company that has greater potential for them. This is called sector rotation. In the financial markets, there are often trends. There have been trends for technology stocks, for biotechs, etc. and when the trend is over, investors cash in their profits, which causes prices to fall, and they position themselves on other more trendy stocks.

A company can make very high profits, but how did it make them? If it laid off staff to reduce its payroll costs, that's not necessarily a good sign. It may also show that the company is in difficulty or that it no longer expects strong growth in the coming months.

Let us take another example that is even more incomprehensible: unemployment figures.

Unemployment increases and financial markets accelerate upwards. This does not seem logical to the apprentice trader who thinks that if there is more unemployment, it is because companies have laid off employees because their order books are empty and therefore economic activity must slow down. Certainly, that makes sense.

But we may also be in a context of strong growth and fear of inflationary pressures. If inflation begins to rise, there is a risk that central banks could raise interest rates, which would cause the financial markets to plummet.

So rising unemployment may also be perceived by the financial markets as a relief. The spectre of inflation is receding, the central banks are not going to raise interest rates and this is ultimately excellent news because investors were focusing primarily on this interest rate issue.

On the other hand, falling unemployment can bring down financial markets and also cause the apprentice trader to misunderstand.

"But what are they doing, unemployment is going down, that's good news, it means the economy is in shape and the financial markets are down, it's a scam! “

That is a childish assumption! Unemployment that falls too sharply can also be a source of concern for investors. Effectively, companies may find it difficult to recruit to grow if full employment is reached.

What happens then? To attract talent, companies are forced to raise salaries sharply. This reduces their margins and, therefore, the dividends that can be paid to shareholders. If we are in a situation of wage pressure, falling unemployment is bad news for investors and stock prices may fall.

What I'm trying to show you with these basic examples is that our interpretation of the numbers is irrelevant. I don’t know how many times I have seen apprentice traders rushing to look for the U.S. unemployment statistic that’s just fallen. I often say to them, without them always understanding me, "Don't go looking for the statistic, it doesn't matter what you think or how you interpret this statistic, look at your charts, you have your answer in front of you".

What is interesting is how the market reacts to these figures and what information it gives us about the problems investors are currently facing.

With these examples, we can see that there is never a scam on the financial markets, there is always an internal market logic. And if the market doesn't think like us, it's not that there's manipulation or that the market is wrong, it's just that we're not in tune with the market.

That is why I don't think that we should analyse statistics when we trade financial markets, we should analyse reactions to the statistics, try to get closer to this group sub consciousness that makes the financial markets fluctuate. The logic of the financial markets is, for me: I'm zooplankton, so it doesn't matter what I think. What's important is what the person who has 10,000 times more capital than I do thinks. He's the one who's going to make the market move.

The financial markets have been increasing in a straight line for 10 years and I think that's stupid? Well, I lower my ego, I stay humble, at my level and I have bought for 10 years because there are people with more capital than me who have decided that everything is fine. I don't trade the financial markets to be right and sooth my failing ego.

The strength of a basic trend can also be judged in a very simple way:

When bad news drives up the financial markets, optimism is the order of the day.

I come to the financial markets to make money as regularly and securely as possible. I have to follow the big guys. Nothing else, everything else is a fairy tale, I stick to my role of zooplankton in the same way that remoras stick to sharks.

14

REVIEW

In this chapter, let's recap to check that you are on the right track before going any further.

These five steps are essential to achieving regular and secure trading.

Having solid foundations then allows you to concentrate on finding your method calmly.

1) The choice of broker and the quality of the feeds provided by your broker

This is a fundamental step, without a good broker and a good trading platform, you have no chance of making money in the long run.

Favour solid players offering good security for your funds, regulated in safe countries and with good financial transparency (listed company and/or regularly published annual accounts).

To be able to trade, you need professional quality data feeds in ticks and not partial feeds, which many brokers offer to save bandwidth at their clients' cost.

These shortened feeds distort your view of the market. Effectively, your technical indicators based on these feeds give you false information. There again, the choice of a broker who offers ticks is essential.

2) The quality of your Internet connection

The quality of your internet connection is important for peaceful trading. Do not hesitate to change your internet provider if you are not satisfied with your internet connection.

I have noticed huge differences between two internet providers in the same apartment!

3) A well-adapted and maintained trading station

Favour a desktop trading station that will be more powerful and responsive than a laptop for the same price.
Maintain your trading station properly and regularly so that it maintains its performance.

4) Secure your trading station and your trading

Think about buying equipment to protect your internet box and your computer from power cuts (inverters for the computer AND the internet box).

Always have a back-up solution (4G smartphone) to place your orders, in case there is an internet outage or if your computer crashes.

5) Do paper trading and keep a trading journal

Discover the world of financial markets with paper trading to familiarise yourself with your trading space and find what seems to gel with you the most (stocks, indices, Forex).

Take as many notes as you can and review them regularly so as to memorise and discover areas for improvement in your trading.

You didn't think I was going to let you start chapter 2 "My Trading Method" without checking that you have integrated everything, did you?

We will progress step by step, slowly BUT surely. Patience is a trader's main virtue.

MY TRADING METHOD

RESEARCH

15

HOW TO FIND YOUR OWN TRADING METHOD

You are now at the research stage. This is a period when you need to store up a maximum amount of experience, "eating charts" for tens, hundreds, maybe even thousands of hours.

Looking back, and I think I'm going to scare you, it took me several years to stabilise my trading method.

Effectively, I lacked consistency more than anything. I decided to follow an indicator, but I didn't test it for long enough. If after two or three weeks I was still making a loss, I got discouraged. And then I'd start all over again with a new indicator and so on. You waste a few years at that rate. So I lacked perseverance.

Worse than that, as soon as I had a losing trade I would tinker with the parameters again to try to find the right setting. This was a big mistake, because in the end, by changing too many parameters, at once, if there was an improvement in my trading, I was unable to determine which setting had contributed to that.

With hindsight, I was in the beginner's phase. I was looking for the miracle indicator that, if perfectly adjusted, could make me a fortune easily and without much effort, of course. I finally buried my search for the philosopher's stone and the miracle indicator.

Discouraged, having not found anything compelling, I then turned to turnkey trading solutions. I started to flit from method to method, each one more complex than the other, but I wanted to get my money's worth. It was my Boeing captain period with indicators flashing all over the place. Good thing I wasn't epileptic!

I realised later that having indicators all over my charts reassured me. It looked very professional after all. I was losing money, but I was getting intellectual satisfaction from it. I could spend hours annotating the divergence brought by a W indicator in agreement with a Z indicator, while of course monitoring the moving average W which was correlated with the B indicator, itself being, otherwise it would not be interesting, a sub-indicator weighted with respect to the volume X. In short, it kept me busy, I had beautiful colours everywhere, I was looking for correlations in all directions, I scattered, I spread out and in the end, I had nothing but intellectual satisfaction.

What was I missing, at that time, to progress in the search for my method?

Above all, I lacked conscientiousness, because I wanted to get results quickly. So, I tended to flit from indicator to indicator, from method to method without ever really taking the time to understand and analyse it.

The worst part is that I was not aware of my lack of conscientiousness, I spent all my evenings "working" on my trading.

Looking back, I wasn't doing anything, I was just playing a video game. I spent my evenings, after not exactly exhilarating days in national education as a history teacher, trading for real on the Nasdaq. And because I was in the markets, placing my orders every night, I felt like I was working and being a trader.

It was like learning to drive, you get in the car and you drive. And I had this flaw about wanting to get on with it, about wanting to trade straight away. You may see yourself in my description, I think many traders have gone through these phases. If through my writing, I can shake you up, and make you gain the few years that I have lost by going around in circles, I will be very happy.

That's not learning to trade, that's having fun, feeling like you're in it, being a trader, being in the markets, searching, etc. but in fact, it's going around in circles and it's not really working.

So what really is working towards finding your method?

Your objectives and intervention strategy must firstly be precisely defined. And then stay focused on your decision, for many months, to be able to progress.

I believe that winning trading, in the short, medium and long term, is based on ultra-specialisation. And that's the mistake of apprentice traders who want to trade everything at once, Forex (let's go to the most complicated market in the world while we're at it), two or three indices and then, because that's going to do well, a little petroleum and, who knows, gold too.

STOP STOP STOP!

I'll be honest, it's a load of rubbish. To be profitable and efficient, you would have to do one method of trading specifically for Forex, a second for stocks, a third for indices, etc. You are already struggling to find a method that works for just one asset. There again, you are living a dream, the quest for the Holy Grail, the universal multi-media method.

To give you a different comparison, it's exactly as if you decided to become a top sportsman in football, fencing, judo and rowing. I wish you the best of luck. With trading, it's exactly the same, you have to choose and specialise. It is better to excel in one area than to be mediocre in several.

How to define an intervention strategy?

To begin with, choices have to be made (and choices always involve giving something up and frustration). It's a good thing you are embarking on the most frustrating activity in the world, defining a method to have a statistical advantage:

Are you going to use fundamental analysis (growth and value) or technical analysis (systematic and discretionary)? A little mix of both? Then again, we can afford the luxury of doing a little of both.

Then you have to determine the appropriate financial solutions: shares, trackers, Forex, Futures, warrants, turbos, options, etc.

Then you choose your instrument: CAC 40, Dax 30, Dow Jones 30, Nasdaq 100, etc. for indices for example.

Finally, choose an investment horizon: scalping, day trading, swing trading, buy & hold.

In my case, and this is what I am going to discuss in the following chapters, I specialised in discretionary scalping on the Dax 30 and the Dow Jones 30 using Futures. I do a little bit of CAC 40 and Nasdaq 100, but that's totally insignificant.

Let me stress once again, you absolutely must specialise. When I was recruited by a Hedge Fund, they were looking for a scalper on the Dax 30. They weren't looking for a multi-product trader.

If you are interested enough to look at recruitment advertisements in the field of trading at banks or hedge funds, you will see that they are all looking for highly specialised profiles.

Manchester United never recruits a marathon running basketball player who does competitive judo into their football team. I know it's tempting, brokers let us trade any stock, any index any commodity with one click. We're like a child in a huge bakery who is only allowed to choose one cake.

Whatever the choice, it is always frustrating and disappointing. Too bad, if you want to be effective in trading, you have to be ultra-specialised. Beyond that, if you really want to come into trading to have fun, to experience sensations, I encourage you to trade everything and to take a good antacid.

After 25 years of trading, I trade, in a different way, two indices. I too would like to trade orange juice, for example, I find it fun. But I'm not here to have fun, I'm here to make cash and the time wasted relearning how to trade orange juice would make me lose money. Effectively, I could use that time to improve my strong points, i.e. scalping on the Dax 30 and the Dow Jones 30.

That's why when beginners ask me why I don't trade X, Y or Z? I say: "I don't need to, I specialise in two indices that I master very well and my objective is to dig even deeper in understanding them".

Anyway, choose, choose and choose.

Map work

Now we can get to the real work, map work. But what is map work?

It's a term that I coined during my coaching sessions to help people understand how the real work, learning trading should be viewed, in my humble opinion.

The first thing is, you have to stop playing video games. If you trade a lot of hours on your demo account, you're testing ideas, you're having fun, but are you really working?

Effectively, you are absorbed by the prices that scroll by at full speed, before your very eyes. You take a position, you exit, you re-enter, etc. you're on the markets, on the front lines, like a soldier fighting. You learn the technical moves for giving orders but you stay in the moment.

To find your trading method, I suggest that you take a step back, move up and become a general.

I realised that you have to work the maps in trading to progress when I learned that Napoleon had planned his battles in advance. He had an intelligence service that mapped, as accurately as possible, the topography of the areas he was going through.

At the time, there were no satellites and survey maps were classified as secret. With his maps, Napoleon had a major strategic advantage. He decided in advance where
he would like to fight and tried to draw the enemy to his ground. When he arrived on the battlefield, he already knew how he was going to position his cavalry, his artillery, etc. while the enemy general was discovering the terrain.

So to find my trading method, I did exactly the same thing. I turned off the video game, I printed out tens, hundreds, thousands of charts. I spent tens, hundreds, thousands of hours looking at these charts. I always walked around with them, I had an hour's break between classes, I took out my charts and studied them, I scribbled on them, etc. I took them everywhere, they were my main reading material. This enabled me to take the time to analyse the maps, the charts.

I wasn't on the front-line in the heat of the moment spending my energy unnecessarily. I was doing real research work, that's how I found all my techniques. I didn't find them by trading, I found them by analysing the maps over the weekend.

What happened then?

I started to spot recurrences. "That's weird, every time the Dax 30 hits its mS2 M pivot point, it seems to bounce back".

I would write down these ideas in a notebook and then I would develop the assumption by printing the same situation over different time units. Sometimes my impressions were wrong, sometimes I found a statistical advantage that I noted.

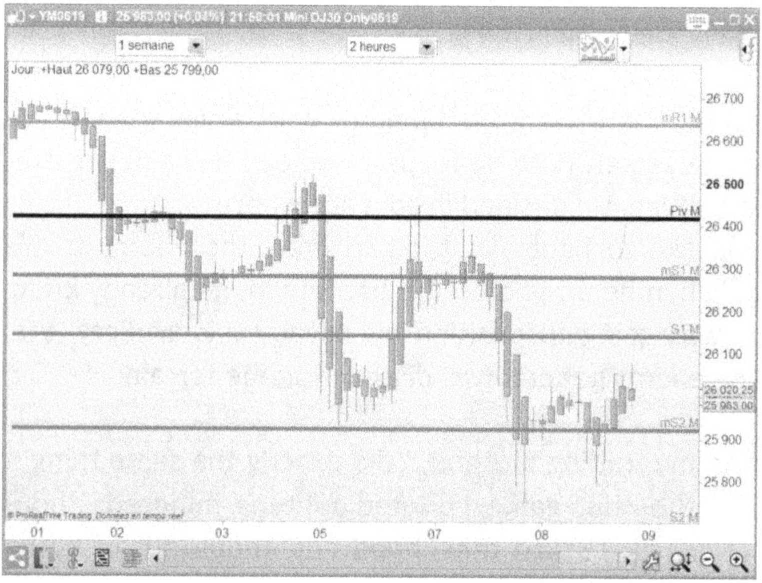

Dow 30 Future over one week for a map study

Proceeding this way has a lot of advantages:

Memory recall is much more efficient when you are analysing charts than when you are trading, your brain has time to memorise price dynamics.

I think you gain more experience because by printing the charts you analyse 10, 15, 20 interesting situations in one hour. In the heat of the moment, you may only get one or two per hour. Therefore, you experience multiple trading situations with hindsight, while being in full control of yourself, without stress, without adrenaline, etc.

You can work all the time, on the underground, on the bus, walking down the street to go shopping, etc. which is not possible if you do the map work on your computer.

Some tips for working with maps

Once you have selected your index, for example, choose a time unit that allows you to view the entire week. It was by visualising the battle on the markets from Monday to Friday that I was able to detect numerous things.

Put one indicator, or two at the most, on your chart. Print out the last three months and you have 12 charts. And look at them. Can you see anything? A recurrence? Yes, write it down. No, drop that indicator.

There are dozens, hundreds of indicators available on our broker trading interfaces. There's no need to hurtle into the latest "trendy" indicator. Test them all. This is the part where you can be curious. But don't waste too much time, if the indicator doesn't speak to you, even if it's trendy, move on to the next one. At some point, you're going to find some indicators that speak to you. They really do speak to you, that is, you will find them logical, obvious.

When I talk about pivots, which are my favourite indicators, sometimes I find it hard to understand that people don't see the same things as I do. It seems so obvious, almost childish. On the other hand, show me a moving average or Bollinger bands, you can spend five days explaining to me how you trade using them, I won't understand anything, they don't speak to me, they don't interest me, I don't "feel" them. You need to start feeling your indices, your indicators.

It's hard to explain, it's like falling in love, and it just comes to you. I was much more intuitive about the logic of indicators, like Darvas' boxes, the pivot points came to me and I had it, it was obvious, everything became clearer, simpler and understandable.

I hope you experience this lightning bolt of clarity, but it won't come by itself. You really have to look, you have to live for charts for hours, days, months.

When you think you have a lead, you explore it by scanning all the time units from XX ticks to minutes, to hours over a maximum of two or three years. I don't think you have to check or backtest for five to ten years, because the market changes and your method evolves with it.

So this is a long job for you to look forward to, but it's an exciting job because you learn a lot more in a few months by map work than in a few years by trading on a demo account.

And think about buying a printer that doesn't have expensive refill cartridges, because they can eat into your budget.

I'm going to let you find your own method and in the next chapter, I'm going to describe my method to you. As you will have understood, as I said in the introduction of this book, it is not a question of you imitating or aping me.

My trading method is adapted to my personality, my problems and my appetite for risk. It is the reflection, if not the fruit, of long personal work over more than a decade that has forged my experience, my vision of trading, my abilities, my relationship to money linked to my past. You do not have the same problems, experiences, desires, etc. as I do. For example, I'm unable to swing trade, which annoys me deeply. Scalping, on the other hand, relaxes me, it's dynamic, you get results quickly and you can move on. It fits my personality perfectly. Waiting for days or months to unlock a position in swing trading, for my personality, is akin to absolute masochism. I hate waiting, I like straightforward, quick decisions.

So remember that there is only one method of trading that can satisfy you, where you will be perfectly comfortable, and that is the one you build for yourself. If you try to get into someone else's habits, no matter what happens you will always be cumbersome and clumsy.

Let other people’s methods be your food for thought. Adapt and modify those methods. In short, custom build your method, it will suit you and you will experience real satisfaction.

16

MY TRADING STATION CHARTS

Chart configuration is a very important step for a trader's comfort and efficiency. You are probably not going to believe it, but it took me more than six months of research and testing to find the chart configuration that offers me maximum efficiency.

Visual comfort, the angle of viewing the charts, the colours used which should not tire the eyes, the size of the chart windows which should not induce an upward or downward bias, the number of candlesticks displayed, etc. all this has been taken into account.

I am going to describe how I arranged this, don't overlook this step. You can't trade with your PC's windows arranged carelessly. It is difficult enough to start trading without adding more difficulties for yourself.

I work with 4 main trading screens so as to have visual comfort and to be able to simultaneously observe variations in the DAX 30, Dow Jones 30, CAC 40 and Nasdaq 100.

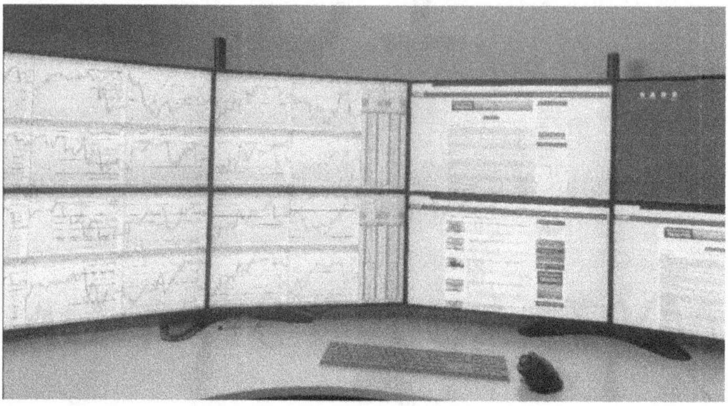

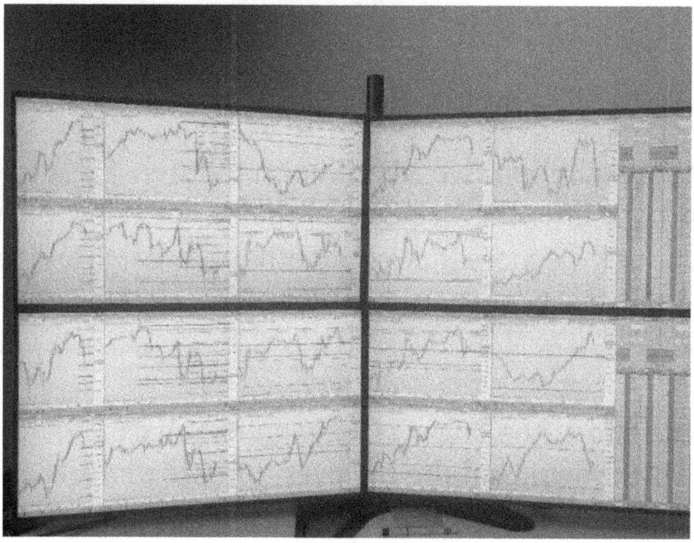

My eight-screen desktop trading station

For each index, I have an open order book, a scalping interface, and 5 charts.

I also have a mobile version for long trips abroad with a 27-inch iMac in a special case that allows my computer to travel in the hold. I arrive at the hotel and in less than two minutes my trading station is set up.

It doesn't sound like much, but it took me years of testing to find a case, strong enough to travel in the hold, custom-made for my iMac and that meets the airline standards in terms of weight and dimensions. In the private area, you can see the characteristics and contact details of the manufacturer if you are interested.

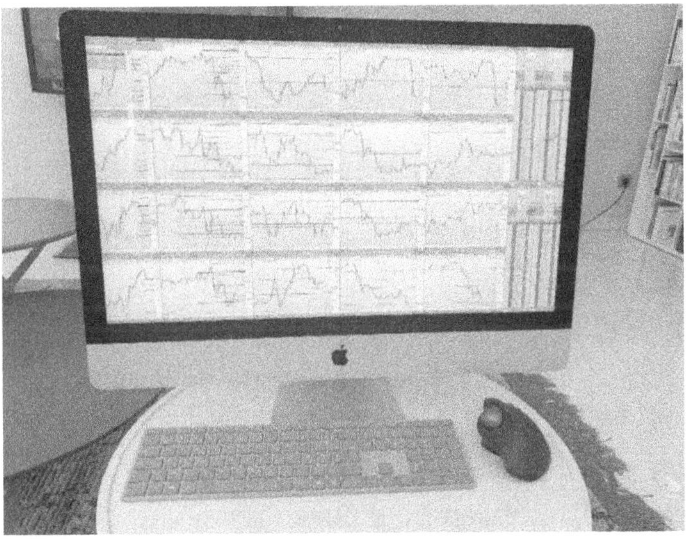

My mobile trading station

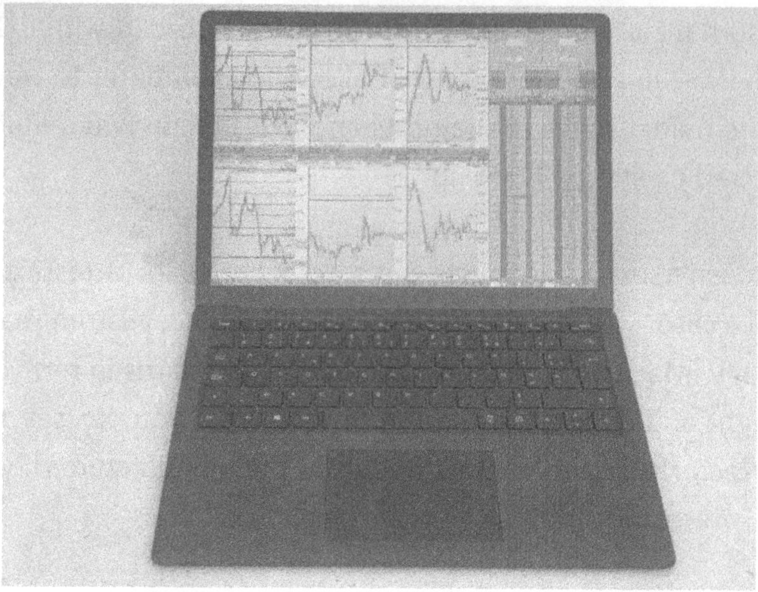

My ultra-mobile trading station

Ultralight and with high autonomy, my mobile trading station is a Microsoft Surface laptop. This enables me to trade outside absolutely anywhere.

You'll notice that whatever the computer, I keep exactly the same layout so as not to lose my bearings and to avoid handling errors. On the laptop, I have exactly the same scalping screen as on the eight-screen trading station. On the 27-inch 5K iMac, the trading station displays all the information I have on my desktop PC on my four UHD displays.

Description of the different windows

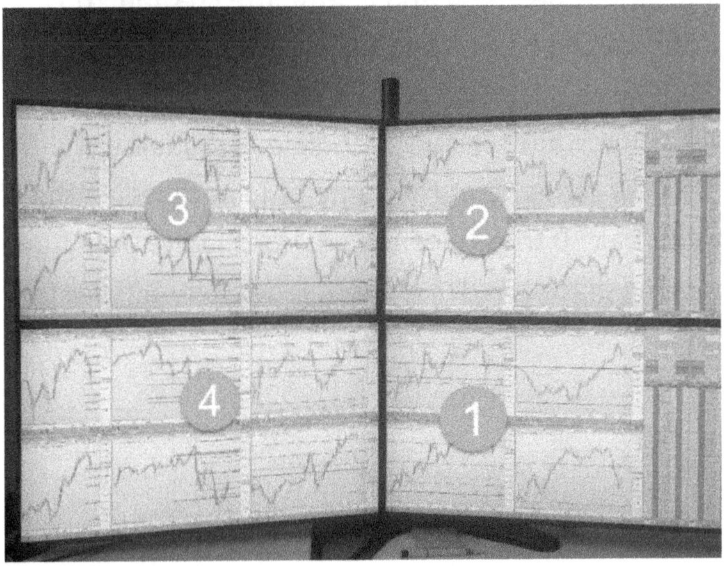

On screen 1:

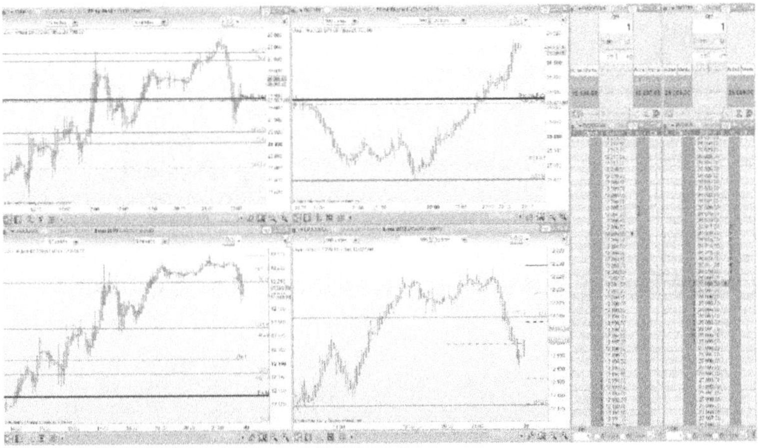

I have the order books for the Dax 30 and the Dow Jones 30 side by side on the right and display the scalping interfaces above them. This enables me to be highly effective at scalping both indices at the same time.

For scalping, I display a chart in 100 ticks in 100 units so I can select my input precisely and a 5-minute chart in 100 units so that I can see the basic trend for my scalping.

It is very important for me to be able to visualise the Dax 30 and the Dow Jones 30 at the same time because, in the afternoon, the Dax 30 tries to echo variations in the Dow Jones 30. This lets me place 1 order on each index very efficiently.

On screen 2:

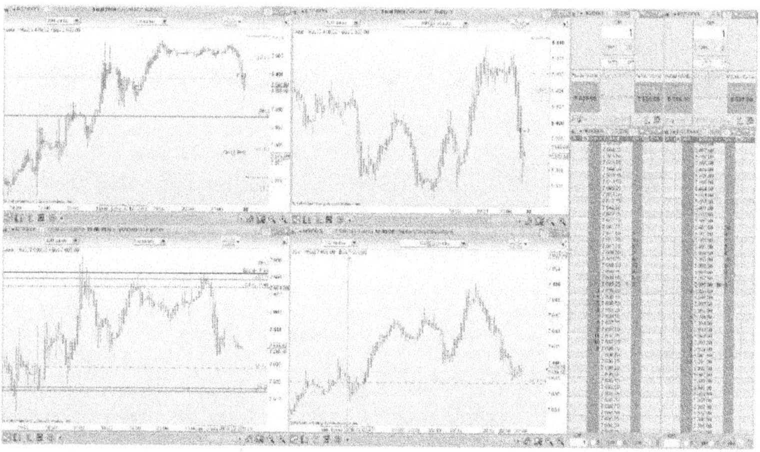

The same layout but with the Nasdaq 100 and CAC 40.

On screen 3 for the Dax 30 and the Dow Jones 30 and on screen 4 for the CAC 40 and the Nasdaq 100:

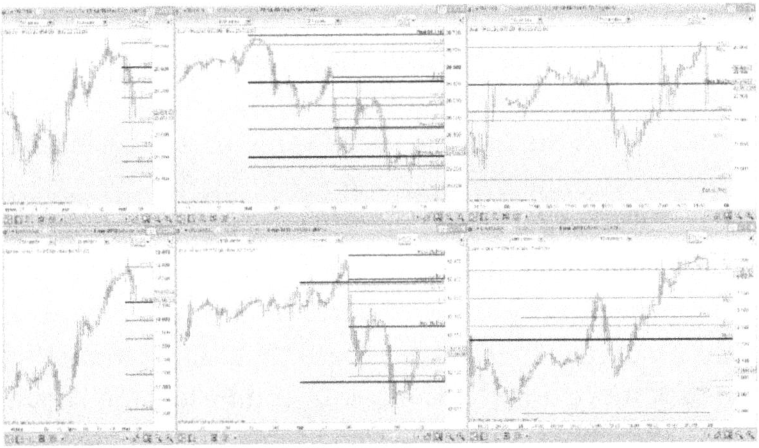

I display 2 charts, 15 minutes and 2 hours in 100 units (which enables me to keep an eye on the whole day on the 15-minute chart and on two weeks on the 2-hour chart). This way I can see at a glance the high and low points of the day for the last 2 weeks. I don't need to extend the time frame, key hindsight is enough.

The last chart is a daily 50 unit chart that I use to see the general trend, I can scan two and a half months of a daily trend at a glance.

For day trading I use the 5-minute chart paired with the 15-minute chart and 100 units of historical data. I also use it as a scalping tool to determine if the trend in 5 minutes is strong or not.

Screens 1 and 2 are therefore dedicated to scalping space.

Screens 3 and 4 are there to take a step back from the situation and spot if a day trading opportunity arises, always keeping an eye on the underlying trend.

Take some time to think about the organisation of your trading station and carry out a lot of tests to display your charts differently. With the ProRealTime Premium trading interface, I can set up absolutely everything.

In this way I can give pivot points a colour, thickness and special colour depending on whether they are monthly, weekly or daily. This way I identify the areas that I find interesting to scalp much more quickly. The colour coding lets me know.

17

A SCALPER IS A SNIPER

I am going to try to describe my trading style as accurately as possible. Again, this is by way of example, I hope above all to provoke some reflection in you, perhaps some questioning or confirmation of your trading style.

I'm basically a scalper which means I like to take trades in high potential areas and cash out my gains quickly. A scalper's philosophy is "a bird in the hand is worth two in the bush". But beware, I don't refuse to do day trading, quite the contrary.

Usually, for me, a day trading opportunity is a scalp that is well on its way and that I quickly secure as soon as it is positive. If it's at +5 +8, and I think there's potential for day trading, I place a TP+1 to ensure at least 1 point of gain and give the product a chance. If it takes off, so much the better, if it ebbs back, I get +1 without any frustration. One of my trading rules is not to lose money and I never let a positive trade turn negative. It's a crime against my wallet.

While for a lot of traders it's a bad trade, they grumble, for me it's an excellent scalp. Effectively, the trade ended up positive and I was able to launch a day trade, which could have made a lot of money, without any risk. That's why I often have 1 point of gain on my trade statements, it's often scalps secured at +1 that I let continue.

Orders — 1 week

Executed

Name	Price	Gain
DAX30 Only0619	12 059,50	150,00 €
Mini DJ30 Only0619	25 789,00	15,00 $
Mini DJ30 Only0619	25 786,00	
DAX30 Only0619	12 053,50	
DAX30 Only0619	12 060,00	150,00 €
DAX30 Only0619	12 054,00	
DAX30 Only0619	12 060,00	125,00 €
DAX30 Only0619	12 055,00	
DAX30 Only0619	12 182,50	12,50 €
DAX30 Only0619	12 182,00	
DAX30 Only0619	12 161,00	12,50 €
DAX30 Only0619	12 160,50	
DAX30 Only0619	12 157,00	137,50 €
DAX30 Only0619	12 151,50	
DAX30 Only0619	12 195,50	37,50 €
DAX30 Only0619	12 194,00	
DAX30 Only0619	12 202,50	25,00 €
DAX30 Only0619	12 201,50	

As you can see on my trade statement, I made 10 trades, 9 on the Dax 30 and 1 on the Dow Jones 30. I only traded at 1 lot because volatility was very high and the market was very jittery.

As soon as the market is jittery and the VIX index increases, I reduce the number of lots to a minimum. My number of lots per position varies according to the current volatility, my state of fatigue and my view of the market. If we get to one of my favourite setups, with high probability, and if the conditions allow it, I use a larger position size.

Scalping is, above all, fluid, permanent adaptation. You can trade at 1 lot for 3 weeks and the following week scalp at 2 to 5 lots.

To follow this fluidity, I don't place any stops. Be careful, I don't place any because, after 25 years of trading, I am able to take my losses without any problem.

Beginners are always advised to place stops of course, as a lot of them can't take their losses. Too much ego. But when you have been in the financial markets for a long time, you've had so many slaps in the face that you no longer have an ego. A little satisfaction at most, when the trading day has been highly positive, but knowing that the next morning you're starting again from scratch.

And you'll see in the following chapters that if I don't place a physical stop, I've always determined the exit zone in advance.

A scalper doesn't give a damn about Bull or Bear controversies. He can be a buyer in the morning and a seller in the evening. He's not on any side. He always foresees both possible scenarios. He's a kind of maverick who doesn't take sides with either the Bears or the Bulls. The only thing he's looking for is a little volatility.

A scalper seeks consistency in his trades

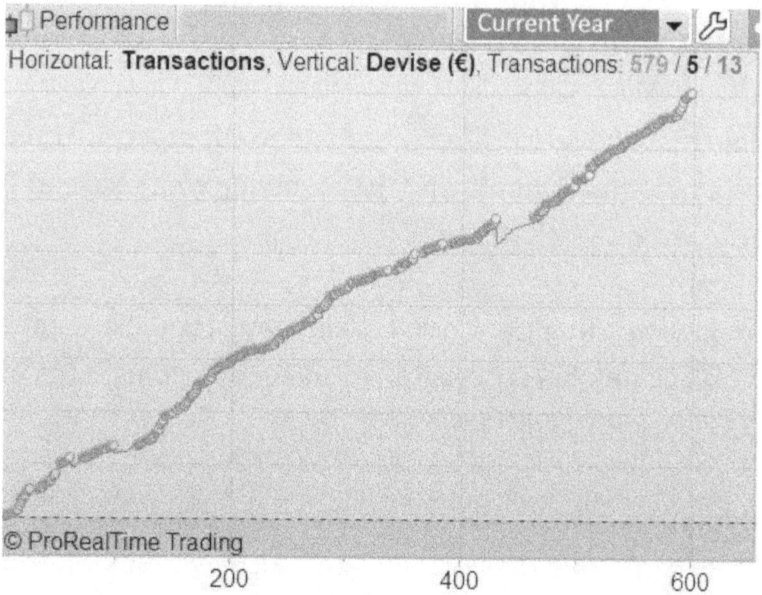

My results from 1st January 2019 to early May 2019

You can immediately see, by looking at my results, that what a scalper is looking for is above all regularity with low Draw-down.

He trades more often than a day trader or a swing trader, but not as often as you might think. My average, since the beginning of the year, is about seven trades a day with a profit factor of 7.17. It is clear that a scalper is above all a sniper, he only intercedes a few times a day but does so with extreme precision.

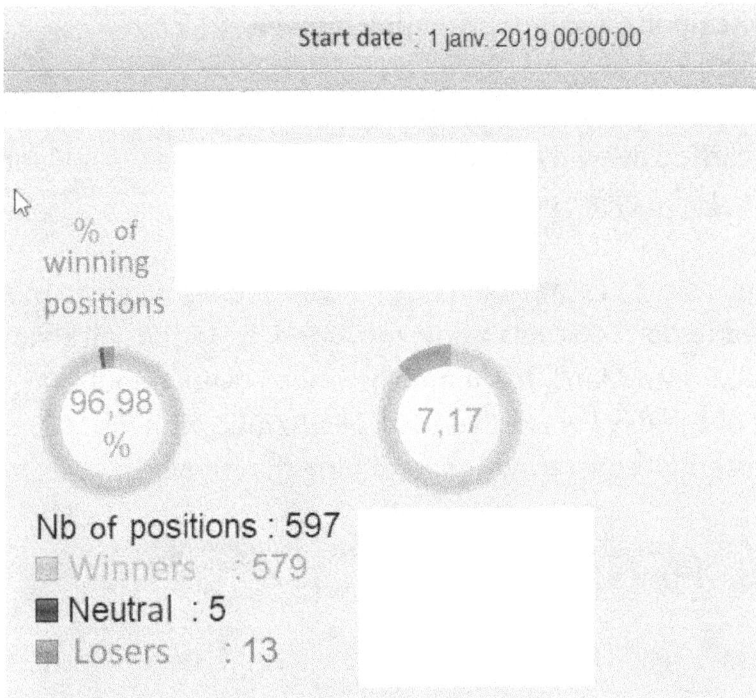

Statistics for the beginning of 2019

A quick word about stock market alarms: they are indispensable to the sniper. During your morning analysis, you identify areas that seem interesting to you, you place alarms before the price gets into the zones that interest you so that you can take action in time. So you don't have to sit in front of your screens for 14 hours a day. Hence the importance of good preparatory work.

His obsession with regularity. He wants to strive for the most perfect equity curve possible. Achieving this consistency requires patience, analysis, and sniper-like composure.

The scalper's a sniper preparing himself

A very common mistake among novice scalpers is that they get carried away by the ease of scalping. They always want to scalp, to be aggressively on the market.

When I started scalping in 2004, I was dealing with too much. I used to do 100 scalps a day, my American friends nicknamed me "Minute Man", the man who scalps every minute. At the end of the day I was exhausted, like Rambo with his M60 machine gun, I constantly shot anything that moved.

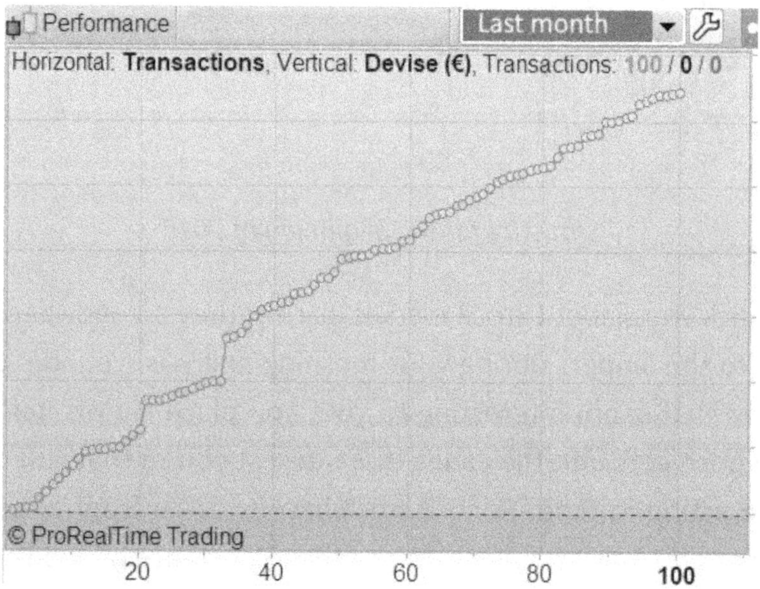

For example, in April 2019 I only did 100 scalps over the month or an average of five scalps per trading day. But I was able to achieve a "Perfect" over the month, something I would have thought impossible a few years ago. In those days, it was not uncommon for me to do 50 to 100 scalps a day. Now, I do that many over a month by selecting the entries extremely precisely.

These are configurations that I have encountered thousands of times before and whose effectiveness I have assessed. So I developed patience above all and I am much more selective in my scalps. Farewell to the meaningless boredom trade that was destroying my trading day.

When he shoots, a sniper must hit the target because he has prepared the ground, nothing is left to chance.

I am in the same state of mind, I consider that scalping is the art of locating zones that have strong potential for a reaction such as weekly and monthly supports and resistances. Like a sniper, a scalper locates the terrain in advance. A scalper's quest is also to take care of his entries. Entering into a quality position is a very likely gain, a decrease in stress because the position will not be in difficulty.

Every morning, before the stock market opens, I start working on the charts. I foresee the different possible scenarios and the zones that I think are interesting for launching operations. I identify in advance the resistance zones, support zones, high and low points of the previous day, the previous week and the previous month. It's my job to spot the trend with no preconceived notions. I predict the three possible scenarios of the day: a rise, a fall or no change.

This preparation stage is usually totally neglected by all novice traders. They go through the market, they start thinking in the heat of the moment. Napoleon won many of his battles by working on his topographical maps. By the time he could choose his battlefield, he had already anticipated all the scenarios, which gave him a strategic advantage.

If you get there, having already foreseen the situation, you are no longer subject to the market, you just have to wait for it to move into an identified zone. Like a sniper, you wait for your target. And when the market moves into your zones, you'll know exactly what you have to do. There's no excitement, there's no adrenaline, there's no approximation, there's no amateurism. You are a professional, you know how to react because you have already planned and thought it through.

To give another, slightly sportier image, a Formula 1 driver knows the circuit in advance, he doesn't discover it during the race. That's exactly what I try to do every morning, identify and plan what I'm going to do when we get to this or that zone. If you don't, you discover the ground during your trading session. You lose efficiency, you increase your stress and your risk of making mistakes. A scalper tries to be constantly in control of the perfect move and it is not a last-minute improvisation.

If you carry out this preparatory work before the markets open, you gain confidence, you are no longer overwhelmed by events because you have prepared all possible scenarios. In the event of a major support break, you already know in advance where the next line of defence for buyers is. You won't be analysing in real-time, rushed by stress and excitement, you have already done the work quietly in the morning while sipping your green tea.

Of course, you don’t control the events but you don’t let yourself be swayed by them at the mercy of the winds, you are in control of what you do. Even if it takes more work, the comfort and quality of your trading can soar. You are no longer the front-line soldier, fighting almost blindly, you have become a strategist who takes a step back from events. It's a much more distanced trading.

My way of trading is extremely simple, I only have five setups. But they're perfectly under control. There is no room for emotion, no room for amateurism, no joy in making money, no pain in losing money. My main goal is to improve myself, not to make money.

A good trading day is a day where I adhere to my money management and trading rules. I'm here to trade as best I can and, for that, you "just" have to be disciplined.

To summarise my trading style:

1) Forward spotting interesting zones in cases of bearish and bullish excesses, of the high and low points of the previous day, the week and the month
2) Always trade with the trend of my time unit (Dow's Law)
3) Do not have a bullish or bearish bias, anticipate all possible scenarios
4) Work less to earn more, limit the number of trades to concentrate on the most profitable ones, work before entering any position
5) Attempt to transform winning scalps into day trading for the most promising ones by securing them with a TP+1

Now, let's look at the indicators I use and the graphical representation of my candlesticks.

18

WHICH INDICES TO CHOOSE FOR SCALPING AND DAY TRADING

Choosing an index is very important for a trader. He needs to find the one that best suits his temperament. I spent hundreds of hours studying different indices to find those that suited me best.

My choice of indices doesn't have to be yours, you need take the time to observe and find out about them. There's no guarantee that you'll fall in love with the Dax 30 the way I did. You may find it too jittery, too noisy, you might need a calmer index like the CAC 40 to demonstrate your trading skills. Be curious, there's plenty of time. And don't hesitate to go beyond your national borders. Just because you're French doesn't mean you "must" trade the CAC 40. Just because you're English doesn't mean you must trade the FTSE

100. Perhaps the Italian FTSE MIB index or the Spanish IBEX 35 index would make you feel most comfortable.

With experience, you could be surprised to find that each index has its own personality, nervousness and history.

In the following chapters, I will try to describe my approach to certain trading configurations or "setups". These are trading techniques that I have developed, that I am constantly trying to improve and that I use on a daily basis.

They are based on a thorough knowledge of the specific nature of each index. And you can only get this "closeness" to your indices by spending a lot of time with them.

So, for the particular technique of Pivot Point scalping, I don't look at it quite the same way if it is the Dax 30 or the Dow Jones 30.

The Pivot Point technique is not a general technique that can be universally applied to all indices. What gives my trading its quality is having particular techniques specific to each index because they are all different.

I suggest that we look at the particularities of the CAC 40, the Dax 30, the Dow Jones 30 and the Nasdaq 100, which are the four indices that I have traded daily for more than a decade. I'm going to add a few words about the S&P 500 and the Euro Stoxx 50 even though I am not a specialist in these two indices.

The CAC 40: is not an index suited to scalping. It's too slow, lacks nervousness and is not impulsive enough. While the Dax 30 takes off on its support, the CAC 40 "waits" a little longer. I don't think there's enough punch for a scalper.

It's a passable index for day trading. But I must confess that I'm not very enthusiastic about this index in day trading. I find it has more qualities for swing trading because it's cheap and you can re-enter several times to work on your unit cost price.

The Dax 30: is the Rolls-Royce of European indices for scalping. It's got it all, it's nervous, it's edgy and it adheres to supports and resistances rather well.

The Dow Jones 30: the Dax 30's twin brother but American style. In other words, it is bigger in everything than the Dax 30. It is more nervous, it is edgier, it is more exciting to scalp but it is much more dangerous. I don't think that the Dow Jones 30 is suitable for a novice trader.

It's an index where you have to be able to take your losses quickly if it's not moving in the right direction. Otherwise, you get slaughtered and the speedometer goes crazy.

For swing trading, it is only interesting for highly capitalised accounts because you need to be able to cash in variations of 400 to 500 points without even batting an eyelid.

At the time of writing, the Dow Jones has a value of 26,000 points. A small variation of 2% against you, which is nothing in swing trading, and you're already over 500 points down.

The Nasdaq 100: I affectionately call it "mad dog". I think it suits it. It is one of the few indices that have the ability to live its life completely unaffected by the rest of the world.

All European indices can be making losses, including the Dow Jones 30 and the S&P 500, the Nasdaq can be making profits. Nothing shocks it.

It is useful to remember that, in this index, we have the famous GAFAMs (Google, Apple, Facebook, Amazon and Microsoft) and that it is, of course, the technology index par excellence on a planetary scale.

It's an index that we can scalp, it's nervous and impulsive. However, it should be handled with care (like all indices that can be scalped).

Personally, my two favourite indices for scalping and day trading are the Dax 30 and the Dow Jones 30.
For swing trading, which I do to a lesser extent, I prefer the S&P 500, the Euro Stoxx 50 and the CAC 40. I find that these are slower and therefore "less scary" indices to hold in a portfolio for a while.

19

MY TRADING INDICATORS

I'm going to tell you about the indicators I currently use for my trading, whether it's scalping, day trading or swing trading and my favourite setups that I have developed over the years.

The indicators I use are the VIX, which let me gauge market tension and potential risks, Pivot Points and ROI.

Trading the VIX, the fear indicator

To better understand the psychological state of the financial markets, it is important to monitor changes in the VIX. Only by observing its value can you quickly assess the "tension" on the financial markets.

Basically, a low index indicates a calm, bullish market. The higher the index, the more nervous the market becomes. A very high VIX should prompt you to be extremely careful.

The VIX indicator, updated in 1993 by the CBOE (Chicago Board Options Exchange), measures the volatility of the US financial market based on the S&P 500. It is calculated daily by the CBOE. This indicator has been very successful in the USA, where it is even possible to trade it.

We call the VIX "the fear index". Its measure of volatility is actually a measure of market nervousness. Effectively, although it was originally developed as an indicator, we now talk about it as an index in its own right.

The VIX is quoted in percentage points. It is intended to approximate changes in the S&P 500 over a 30-day future period, which is then annualised.

Other volatility indices, indexed to other stock market indices, have also been created, such as the VNX, which measures volatility on the NASDAQ 100 or the VXD, which measures the volatility on the Dow Jones 30 index. But the benchmark for volatility is still the VIX.

As the VIX is trademarked by the CBOE, some platforms may have an alternative name for this index such as the “US Volatility index” or something similar.

Creation of the VIX

Historically, the first to officially develop a volatility index were Professors Menachem Brenner and Dan Galai in 1986. Their research on the volatility index was then published under the title "New Financial Instruments for Hedging Changes in Volatility" in 1989. The volatility index was then called the "Sigma index". Its creators intended it to be used as an underlying index for financial derivatives like futures or options.

The CBOE, together with Professor Robert Whaley, began research in 1992 with the aim of creating a volatility index that could be traded, with the particularity of being indexed to the price of options.

In 1993, Professor Whaley presented his volatility index, which he called the VIX. He then put forward a VIX based on data from January 1986 to 1993.

How to trade the VIX

All technical analysis tools can be used on the VIX price. So if you're a fan of technical analysis you are free to perform the graphical analysis of the VIX.

The VIX can be used in different ways:

Firstly, you can use the VIX as part of your money management. The point here is to use the VIX as a risk indicator. If during a period of normal volatility, you take 2 lots, a high VIX can lead you to do less than planned and only take one lot.

Effectively, as volatility is high, the risk is also high. So a single batch is enough to avoid endangering your wallet.

Secondly, you can trade the VIX with derivatives such as options or futures. Since 24 March 2004, it has been possible to trade the VIX with Futures. It was not until 2006 that the VIX was tradable on options.

In under five years, options and futures transactions on the VIX have reached more than 100,000 contracts per day. Beware, a lot of Brokers offer to trade on the VIX, but some offer you their own volatility indices.

Finally, you can speculate directly on the VIX by taking advantage of the normal market rhythms. The periods between 15 July and 15 August and between Christmas and New Year's Day are known to be rarely volatile. If at the end of these periods, the VIX is high, you can take a short position on the VIX (you then sell the volatility) hoping for a fall in the VIX price due to the decrease in volumes that should follow. But in the financial markets, as you know, nothing is certain.

How to interpret the VIX

By analysing the VIX's history, we can discern:

A VIX level between 10 and 15 means that the market is moving in a climate of confidence with low volatility. It is therefore normally bullish. Never forget that financial markets are structurally bullish.

A VIX level between 20 and 30 means that the market is volatile (nervous), but it can be bullish.

A VIX level above 30 indicates very high volatility. We will certainly witness a sharp fall in prices or even a major crisis.

The most important thing about this index is not its actual level, but its variation. It is actually the variations that tell us the changes in the market participants' morale:

When they're pessimistic, the VIX goes up.
When they are optimistic, the VIX drops.

Between 1990 and 2013, the VIX only closed above 40 six times:

44.28 in August 1998: monetary and financial crisis in Russia
39.69 in September 2002: Enron affair
79.13 on 24 October 2008: subprime crisis
40.95 on 7 May 2010 Greek crisis
43.05 on 19 August 2011: sovereign debt crisis
42.96 on 30 September 2011: continuation of sovereign debt

We can, therefore, see that the VIX clearly shows the phases of tension and crisis. Personally, I use it this way in my money management:

Less than 20: batch size unchanged
Between 20 and 30: lot size halved as a precautionary measure
Between 31 and 39: lot size divided by 4 as a precautionary measure
Above 40: I eat popcorn and let the big players wipe each other out. I'll be there the next day, for them, it's not a given.

If you want to investigate further:

How to calculate the VIX

$$\sigma^2 = \frac{2}{T}\sum_i \frac{\Delta K_i}{K_i^2} e^{RT}\ Q(K_i) - \frac{1}{T}\left[\frac{F}{K_0} - 1\right]^2$$

The VIX Formula

Where,

- σ^2 is the VIX

- F corresponds to Futures on S&P 500, which it would represent at maturity
- r represents the risk-free rate
- Ki is the strike price of the option
- K0 represents the first price below the level of the index F
- Q(Ki) is the average price between the bid and the ask of option i
- T represents the maturity
- ΔK_i represents the interval between two strike prices = [K(i+1) -K(i-1)] /2

The RSI

The RSI (Relative Strength Index) is a technical indicator widely used by traders. Therefore, it is best to understand it, master it and perhaps integrate it into your trading. At least that's what I'm doing. It's mainly useful to me in 5-minute and 15-minute timeframes for day trading.

Definition of the RSI

The RSI is a technical indicator invented by J. Welles Wilder. He first described it in *New Concepts in Technical Trading Systems* in 1978.

It enables us to determine two things:

1) To see the strength of a **trend** (and spot if the movement is running out of steam)

2) To show whether the market is overbought or oversold.

How is the RSI calculated?

The complete RSI formula is: RSI= 100 - [100/(1+H/B)]

Where:
H is the average of the increases during the last X Time Units (TU).
B is the average of the decreases during the last X TU.
X= the value of the RSI.
Rest assured that the RSI is calculated automatically by all trading software, so you don't have to take out the calculator as J. Welles Wilder did.

On the other hand, be careful, **you can find 3 different RSIs depending on the calculation of the averages** because there are several variants to calculate the averages (exponential average, arithmetic average, etc.).

What you need to understand about RSI:

If you use an RSI 9 on a 2-minute chart, the RSI number will be the average of the last 18 minutes (9*2=18) (so logically, if you buy, you are ready to hold your position for between 2 and 18 minutes).

If you use an RSI 14 on a 5-minute chart, the RSI number will be the average of the last 70 minutes (14*5=70).
If you use an RSI 25 on a 1-day chart, the RSI number will be the average of the last 25 days (25*1=25), (if you buy, you are ready to invest for between 1 and 25 days).

How to use the RSI in trading

The RSI indicates a number between 0 and 100.

An RSI 50 indicates that the market is finding its balancing point on the timeframe that you trade.

When the RSI is above 70, the market is said to be overbought and is a candidate for a bearish correction (this is a possibility, not a certainty) on your time unit.
When the RSI is below 30, the market is said to be oversold and is a candidate for an upward correction (again this is a possibility, not a certainty) in your timeframe.

That's the theory put forward by J. Welles Wilder.

For example, some traders adopt the following RSI strategies:

They start selling when their RSI exceeds 70 AND then crosses back below 70 (a sign that a decline or profit taking is underway).

They start buying when their RSI goes over 30 AND then crosses back over 30 (a sign that an increase may be in progress).

Be warned that trading automatically in this way does not guarantee success because:

The RSI depends on the timeframe you are looking at.

For the same stock or index you can, for example, have a result of 80 for an RSI in 5 minutes, 50 for an RSI in 15 minutes and 23 for a daily RSI.

In conclusion, your index or stock might be overbought in 5 minutes, normal in 15 minutes and oversold on a daily basis. The timeframe is, therefore, a deciding factor! People tend to sell in 5 minutes and buy on a daily basis.

When talking about the RSI, you should always specify the timeframe and the parameter used.

For example, saying that the 5 minute RSI is at 30 doesn't mean anything.

If you say that the 5 minute RSI(14) is at 30, that has meaning.

Effectively a 5 minute RSI(20) will not be 30 but 60, for example, which changes everything.

The limits of the RSI

The RSI works pretty well when you have found the right setting for you: in fact, each index or stock has its own volatility as each trader can be a scalper, a day trader or a swing trader, so you have to adapt this to your particular case.

I often read that J. Welles Wilder advised RSI 14 and so everyone follows this blindly. He suggested this in 1978, in a market with no volatility for stable shares and with a long-term perspective.

My view of the RSI

The RSI is, therefore, a technical indicator developed more than 30 years ago for a stock market that no longer exists, (financial markets are of a volatility and complexity that the author of the RSI could not have imagined at the time). It is, therefore, necessary to try to adapt the RSI to the current market, which is much more nervous than when the RSI was invented.

Why use the RSI if it's outdated?

Simply because it is undoubtedly, like **Pivot Points**, the most used technical indicator by traders.

If X million users have their eyes riveted on the RSI (at 14 of course) then it has an influence on price fluctuation. We don't use it for its own qualities, but because everyone uses it and therefore it is efficient because **the RSI becomes "self-fulfilling"**.

So you have to do tests to define which RSI (9, 14, 17, 25, etc.) suits you best for a specific timeframe (15 minutes, 2 hours, 5 days, etc.).

Each index or stock may, therefore, have a different RSI, each trader a different time unit. So you need to test it using historical prices and check with the actual one. It's work, but it can pay off.

Finally, you don't just need to have the RSI as an indicator. For example, in a strongly bullish market, the daily RSI can stay above 70 for days or even weeks. Conversely, it can stay under 30 for entire days.

Some tips and tricks for the RSI

In general, a scalper takes an RSI 14 in a short TF (1 2 3 minutes). It would be an "explosive" RSI if it highlighted each fluctuation.

Although being a scalper, I don't use it in short TFs because it's too volatile for me. I prefer to follow Dow's law in Heikin Ashi in 100 ticks for "explosive" scalping.

On the other hand, in day trading, I find RSI 14 relevant for validating a rebound phase. Then I use it for the 15 minute timeframe.

The RSI 14 is usually configured with 30 / 70 limits.
To make it less sensitive, I use 25 / 75 in day trading. I prefer to have fewer signals but of better quality.
Of course, the RSI alone will not give a signal to buy or sell. You must decide this according to the context! It is an indicator for me as its name implies, nothing more, nothing less.

It can just comfort me when I think that the market might bounce back suddenly on a detected support, for example.

My favourite combo with the RSI

When we get to a major support, and rebound off it (ideally after having moved beneath it), for a first run / as a test of this support, that Dow's law seems to move into Heikin Ashi over the first 100 tick candlesticks then 5 minutes and that the RSI 14 signal in 15 minutes comes back to cut the 25 level from the top, this is a combo that I would try in day trading.

Here we have the perfect combo for me.

09 May 2019

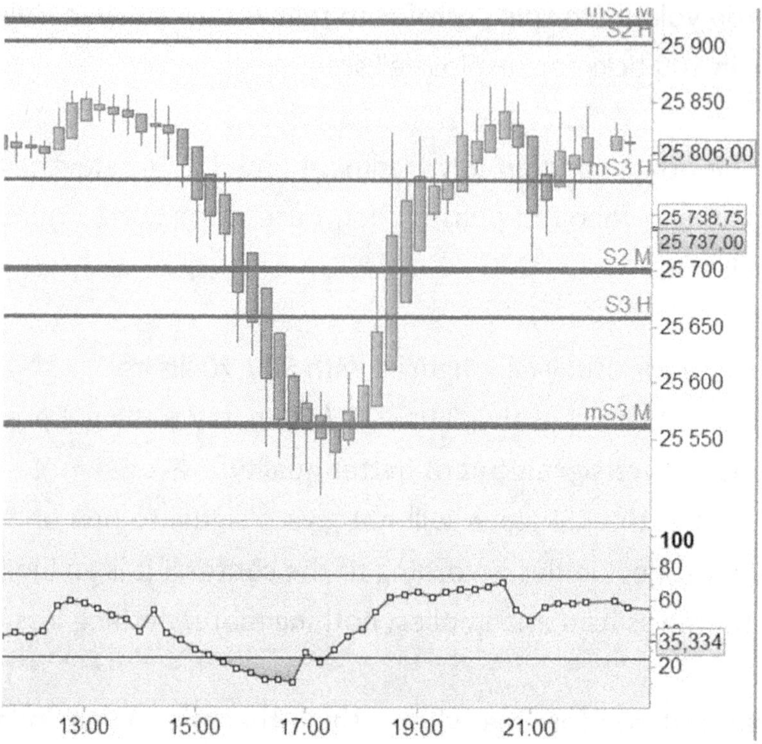

Index: Dow Jones 30 Futures
UT 15
RSI in 25 /75
Support on m S3 M

Analysis:

Reversal of polarity in Heikin Ashi in conjunction with the RSI which goes back above 25 and Dow's law which works for 1 and a half hours.

Potential for 200 points.

Comforted by the fact that the Dax 30 reacts in exactly the same way.

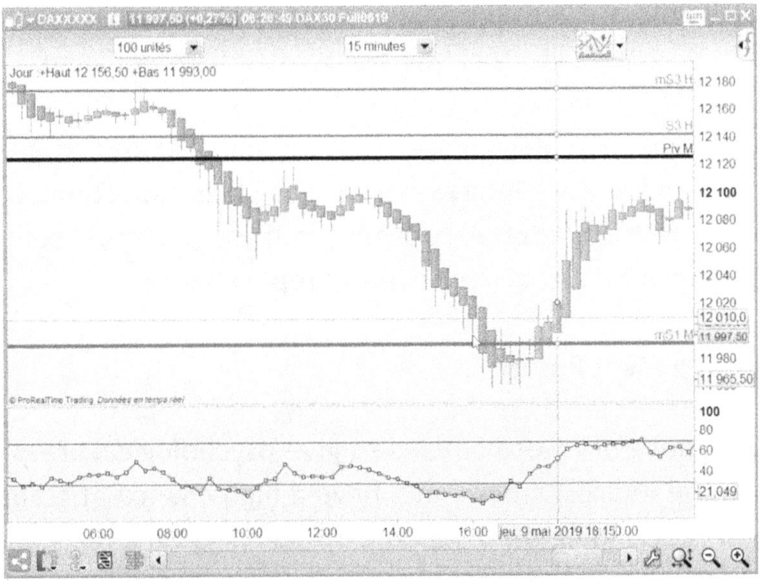

This type of configuration is really "perfect".

Summing up
The RSI shows the strength and speed of the market in one direction. When the RSI is high, it shows that a slowdown in the up-trend may be near and the market may be descending again. It's kind of like throwing a rock in the air. The higher it goes up, the more the velocity decreases, the slower it rises, but it still rises. Once the speed reaches zero, the stone will fall. A high RSI just tells you that the stone is likely to climb more and more slowly, not that it will necessarily fall. This indicator should not be used as the only reason to enter the market, that is doomed to failure.

Pivot Points

Pivot Points are a traditional technique of financial markets operations that I like for their simplicity and effectiveness.

Pivot Points (PP), Resistances (R1, R2, and R3) and supports (S1, S2, and S3) are impressive for the clear indications they can give to the **trader**. Algorithms, in my experience, comply with them statistically far beyond simple chance.

What is a Pivot Point?

The purpose of Pivot Points is to give psychological areas on which the indices, stocks, etc. have a high chance of stabilising, of rebounding off a support or declining on a resistance. Intellectually, it doesn't make much sense, but since a lot of investors use the Pivot Point technique, it does make sense.

This is the principle of self-fulfilment. Obviously, they are also integrated into numerous algorithms where you see the high and low points of certain days that sit right on these areas.

How are Pivot Points calculated?

There are several formulas for calculating Pivot Points, Resistances and other supports. I will show you the most traditional, most used, and therefore, as a side effect, the most effective.

Pivot = (H + B + C) / 3
S1 = (2 x Pivot) - H
S2 = Pivot - (H - B)
S3 = B - 2x (H - Pivot)

R1 = (2 x Pivot) - B
R2 = Pivot + (H - B)
R3 = H + 2x (Pivot - B)
S1, S2 and S3 are the 3 Supports
R1, R2 and R3 are the 3 Resistances

Where H is the previous day's high, B is the previous day's low, and C is the closing price. Don't worry, your trading software will calculate this for you without any problems.

Other Pivot Point formulas

Here you have the formulas for Camarilla Pivot Points and Woodie Pivot Points, the most famous.

A variant of the traditional Pivot Point calculation: Pivot = (H + B + C + O) / 4 or Pivot = (H + B + O) / 3 where O = the highest of the day (so it is a progressive calculation during the day).

I can tell you, it is very useful for trading when there is a very strong, directional trend. When pyramid trading during a strong trend, it gives you appropriate profit stop levels.

What timeframe should be used for Pivot Points?

Usually Pivot Points, resistances and supports are used on daily TFs, for day trading, which makes sense. For example, a rebound on the R1 support is anticipated to return to the Pivot Point. Of course, the context is fundamental in assessing whether R1, R2 or R3 are more likely to block a decline.

With scalping, these levels are also important if the market stabilises on a resistance or a support. You can then scalp on the micro-variations in the defined area. It is, however, more delicate with **scalping** because you have to take into account the period of the day, a stabilisation between 2 pm and 3 pm is more likely to last on a support or a resistance (waiting for the American market) than at 9:30 am when the market is trying to find its levels, which is more dangerous for scalping.
For day trading, I like the weekly and monthly levels which are responsive.

For swing trading, monthly levels are very effective (especially when applying the first pass and buy under the support technique).

Pivot Point strengths

One of the great strengths of Pivot Points is that the levels are determined before the price opens, so they enable you to establish a trading plan, to immediately and simply identify the areas of tension for the day's trading. It is then enough to put alarms at these key levels so that you are warned when prices are approaching these psychological areas.

Pivot Points can, therefore, be used to do some effective preparatory map work.

Pivot Point limits

The levels determined by Pivot Points work particularly well in a calm market or a steady trend (bullish or bearish). If there is a very bad announcement, for example, S1, S2 and S3 supports will not last long and if there is a crash, they are not effective.

As the market generally has a calm trend, they are therefore useful 90% of the time. You can pair them with the VIX to determine if the period is favourable for their use.

Some ideas for Pivot Points

Note, however, that when S3 is broken in intraday, there is a high probability of getting back to that support unless there's a major crash. Similarly, an S3 hit on a monthly time unit is often a rare opportunity to open a long trading position.

I advise you, even in day trading, to display the daily and weekly pivots simultaneously, if the price reaches S1 in daily and S2, for example in weekly, this reinforces the possibility of a rebound.

I use the monthly, weekly and daily Pivot Points as well as the Middles. The Middles are the intermediate Pivot Points, midway between two pivots. I also use the 4-hour pivots but with much less regularity. What I'm interested in is the "reinforcement" they can give to another support. All this will be discussed in detail in another chapter entitled "Scalping Pivot Points".

Pivot Points conclusion

It is often the simplest things that work best. Pivot Point uses can be multiple: determination of a possible rebound area (therefore buying) with the support, or a resistance area (therefore selling or profit taking).

Anyway, I think you need to study them, monitor them, you'll see that the market very often follows them. And if they don't speak to you, don't force your nature and move on to another indicator that pleases your eyes because it does "speak" to you.

20

HEIKIN ASHI AND DOW'S LAW

I use the graphic representation of candlesticks in Heikin Ashi because it smooths the volatility and lets me hold my position in the trend for longer. And I use it with Dow's theory/law.

I find that the two together form a formidable team for trend monitoring and trend entry. It's my favourite combo!

I also rely on Dow's law to open a scalping position in 100 ticks and 5 minutes when day trading.

The simplicity of my trading and setup may surprise you. They are the end result of a long process of analysis to keep to the essentials, following the trend and the price, listening to the market breathe with as little interference as possible.

What is Heikin Ashi?

The Heikin Ashi is a type of chart, developed by Yasuiji Yamanaka, a Japanese **trader**. With this chart, visualising trend intensity is more pronounced.

It is a variant of the **Japanese candlestick chart**, removing some irregularities. To remove these irregularities, calculated averages are used. Using the same model as a **Japanese candlestick chart**, we have 4 variables to construct a Heikin Ashi chart:

Highest, Lowest, Opening price, **Closing price**

The Heikin Ashi formula

Closing Heikin Ashi (closing HA) = (open + high + low + close)/4

Regular candlestick averages are used to calculate the closing HA.

Opening Heikin Ashi (opening HA) = (opening HA from the previous bar + closing HA from the previous bar)/2

The opening HA is the mid-point of the previous Heikin Ashi bar.

How to use the Heikin Ashi

The Heikin Ashi can give us 5 different indicators:
A bullish trend is shown by a green candle.

A strong bullish trend is shown as a green candle with no lower shadow.

A trend reversal is shown by a candle by a small body with upper and lower shadows.

A bearish trend is shown by a red candle.

A strong bearish trend is shown as a red candle with no upper shadow.

Is the Heikin Ashi suitable for scalping?

The Heikin Ashi has highly valuable qualities for **scalping**, particularly for trend reversals on short **TFs** as we can see on this chart:

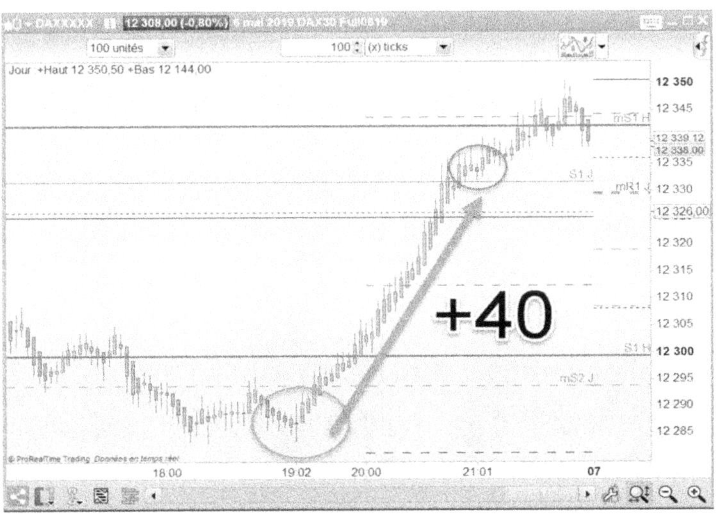

Example of **scalping** with Heikin Ashi on the Dax 30

It enables you to hold your scalp position longer on a volatile index such as the Dax 30 Futures with a small preference for 100 ticks at the moment.

I want to make it clear that this is at the moment that I am writing because trading is about constant adaptation. Two years ago I preferred 21 ticks, for example, because the volatility was lower.

Is the Heikin Ashi suitable for day trading?

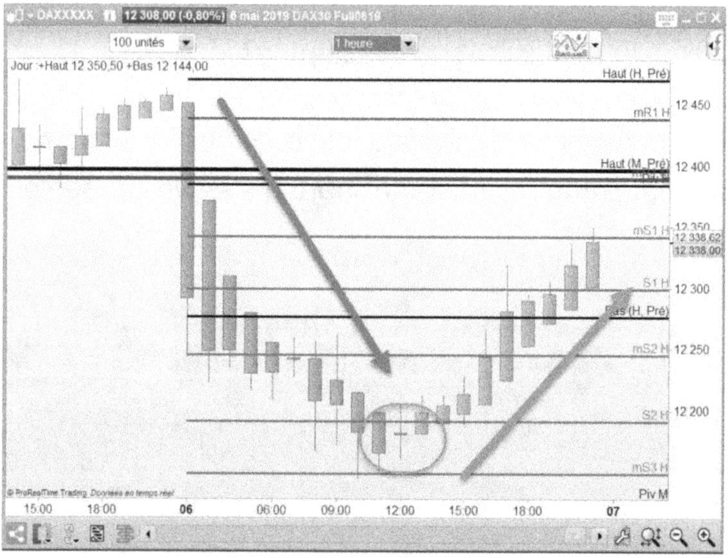

Example of **day trading** with Heikin Ashi on the Dax 30
For timeframes, such as 1 hour, it is very effective, as you can see on this chart.

Is the Heikin Ashi suitable for swing trading?

Yes, the Heikin Ashi is particularly adapted to long-term swing trading with daily, weekly and monthly timeframes.

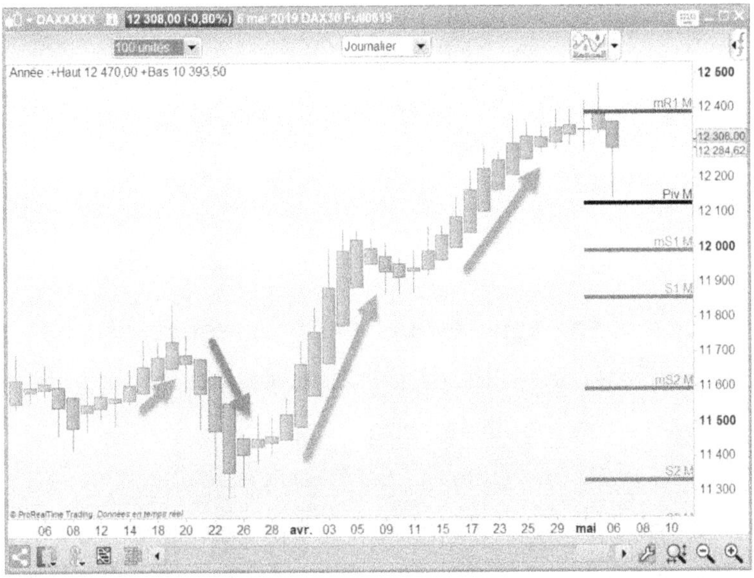

Example of **swing trading** with Heikin Ashi on the Dax 30

Because its results are smoothed, it highlights the general trend and points out areas of uncertainty, like Bollinger Bands do when they are tightened.

Conclusions about the Heikin Ashi

Heikin Ashi is an interesting way to display the price because it favours the trend's perspective and "refines" the more volatile indices. Personally, I love its representation of price, I find it more particularly adapted to the volatile indices like **the Dax 30 and the Dow Jones 30.**

But where the Heikin Ashi develops its full potential is by using it with Dow's law.

Dow's theory

I like Dow's theory so much, I call it Dow's law. This law is based on an extremely simple principle based on observing candlesticks:

If the tops of the candlesticks are progressively higher and higher and the bottoms of the candlesticks are higher and higher, we are in a bullish trend.

If the bottoms of the candlesticks are progressively lower and lower and the tops of the candlesticks are lower and lower, we are in a bearish trend.

If the candlesticks do not follow either of those statements, we are in a period of indecision and we should not go back into the markets.

With traditional candlesticks and Japanese candlesticks, Dow's theory works fairly well, over long time units. For swing trading, they can be used with daily or weekly time units for example.

But I suggest you try Dow's law with candlesticks in Heikin Ashi on very short time units, 100 ticks for scalping and five minutes for day trading.

In this case, we have an association that I find explosive on volatile indices like the Dax 30 and the Dow Jones 30.

So, for this example, we only have this rebound of the Dax 30 with a maximum potential of 50 points in a straight line, by following the Heikin Ashi candlesticks and associating them with Dow's law.

I unconditionally have all my charts in a Heikin Ashi representation from the shortest unit in 100T up to the 5-minute, 15-minute, 2-hour and daily timeframes.

21

SCALPING PIVOT POINTS

I am going to tell you my views on Pivot Points. I use monthly, weekly and daily Pivot Points.

I also display the intermediate levels, which we call the mid-points. These levels are interesting, they are often support points when there is a gentle trend.

I only put the four-hour Pivot Points on my 100 ticks chart. I don't rely on them to trade, they're not decision-makers, but they give me some information such as why the price is stagnating in a particular area.

If you spend thousands of hours in front of your screen looking at your charts, you will notice that Pivot Points "attract" prices. They are often the high and low points of the day.

But more than that, it's the major area in a range that always supports important Pivot Points.

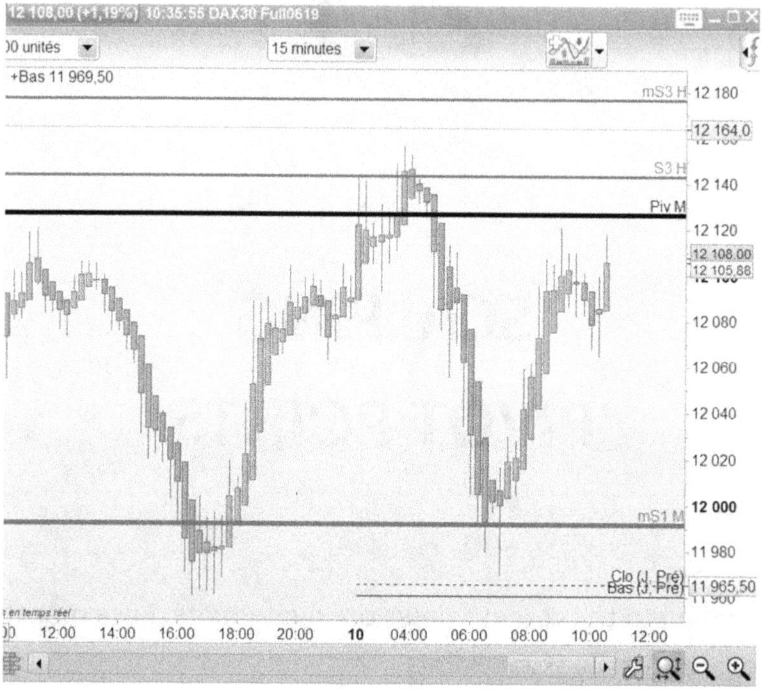

For 24 hours, the Dax 30 has been undulating between its mS1 M and its Pivot M + S3 H. A great range that you can't understand if you don't have the Pivot Points in front of you.

Having patience, and patience is the trader's number one weapon, waiting for the price to hit the Pivot Point and bounce back is often very lucrative. Let's not forget, that's what we're here for.

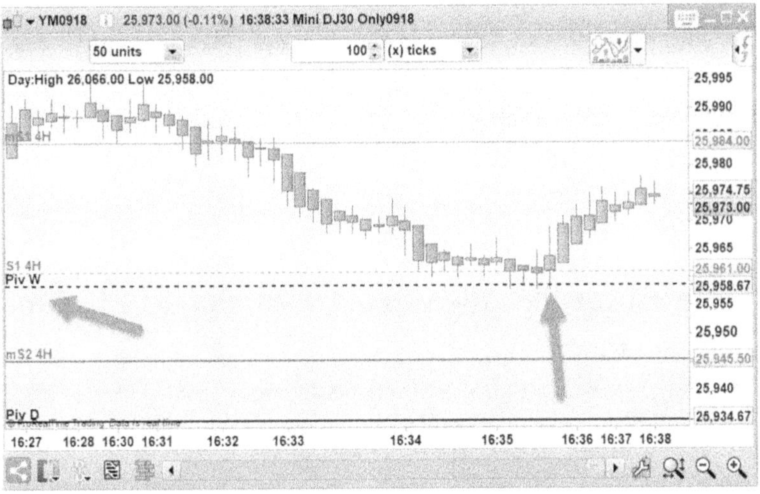

Order list Pending Orders: 0 | 2 days | Filter orders...

Executed | Pending orders | Canceled/Rejected | Multiple-leg | All

Ticker	Qty	Price	Gain
YM0918	-20	25,970.00	€456.2
YM0918	20	25,964.70	
DAX0918	-1	12,004.00	€37.5
DAX0918	1	12,002.50	
DAX0918	-1	12,004.50	€100.0
DAX0918	1	12,000.50	
DAX0918	-2	11,990.50	€112.5
DAX0918	1	11,987.00	
DAX0918	1	11,989.50	

For this trade, I waited an hour for the Dow Jones 30 Futures to bounce back on its weekly Pivot Point.

I re-entered at 20 ATP lots, or $100 per point, aggressively, which explains why my AAC is 25m964.70. To absorb my order of 20 ATP batches, I broke 25m964 in the order book. A few seconds later I resold for a profit after converting €456 into dollars.

This is an example of scalps made by a sniper:

1) We locate the area we are interested in (the map work is essential in the morning

2) we wait

3) the price moves into the desired area and, if it is a major support, we shoot

In those three lines, you have just experienced an hour of scalping.

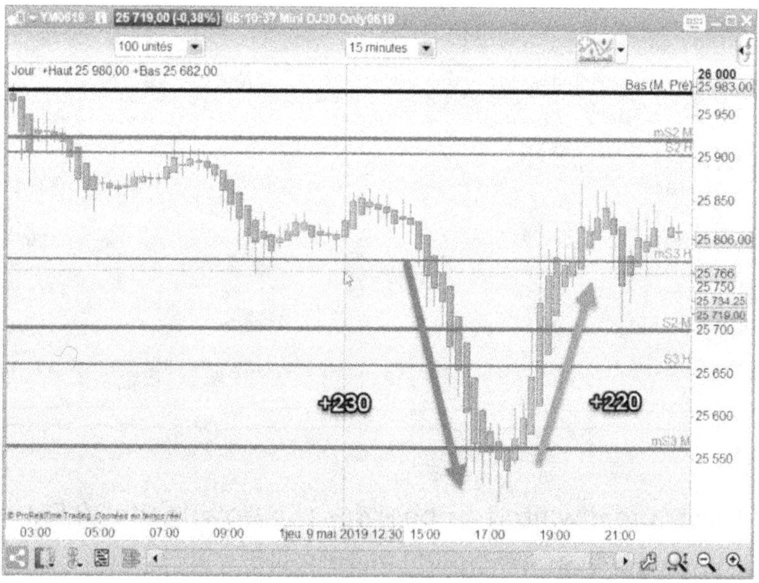

Also, keep in mind, that when the market collapses quickly and violently, it will always stop at a major support.

Why?

Because on the major supports we have scalpers, day traders and especially managers, swingers who take a little dip to improve their AAC. So, everyone is on the lookout, all categories of traders are there, to watch out for a rebound and, understandably, to take advantage of it.

Similarly, when there are fairly clear bullish or bearish trends, Pivot Points often act as resistances or supports. Prices don't ever stop in the middle of nowhere

Pivot Points hierarchy

Not all Pivots are the same. Some are more effective than others because there are more traders on them.

Monthly Pivot Points are the most responsive as all traders are on the lookout at these levels.

Next in the hierarchy, according to my experience and feelings, the monthly midpoints are more effective than the weekly Pivot Points. Weekly Pivot Points are useful enough for day trading and they are as effective as daily Pivot Points for scalpers.

This hierarchy is important because it effects the probability of rebound and the possibility of optimizing its return. For example, on a monthly Pivot Point, I can place between two and six batches depending on market configurations.

On weekly Pivot Points, I'll place between two and three lots. And on daily Pivot Points, I'll usually place between one and two batches. This is what Pivot Points are all about: modulate your trading intensity and use leverage depending on their value.

Of course, as in all things in trading, nothing is absolute, there are always special cases.

In the example I gave you earlier, I traded 20 lots on a weekly Pivot Point. But at that moment, relative to the price history, the probability of a rebound at this weekly level was at least equivalent to a monthly Pivot Point.

Basic Pivot Point techniques

There are some obvious points that are always good to remember: we always buy under a support and we always sell above a resistance.

These are two laws that are absolutely inviolable. Deviate from these laws and you are ostracized among scalpers. These are the tablets in the Law of Scalping. You will see in future chapters why this is so important.

A scalper, therefore, uses his qualities: patience, frustration management and the desire for the perfect movement.

What matters to scalpers is a perfect entry.

"A good scalp in the right place is an assured gain," asserts an American scalper's motto. This quest for perfection, for the perfect, almost obsessive movement, brings scalpers closer to the philosophy of Japanese traders.

For Japanese traders the important thing is not the amount that is going to be gained but the move that was made to enter and exit the position.

For a Japanese scalper, taking a scalp and cashing in 4 points and seeing the price rise by 40 points is not perceived as a bad trade. On the contrary, it is experienced as a perfect trade, extremely secure because he had a margin to take his profits. A European trader is not satisfied with that, he will moan, sob because he doesn't think about the fact that he took four points with almost no risk, he thinks about the 36 points he didn't get.

And that's the difference between a scalper and another trader. There's a whole philosophy of life that's totally different.

A scalper looks for a type of harmony in his trading, he wants his trading to be calm, serene, fluid and, when he and his trading have all these qualities, money will come in.

A "traditional" trader comes to the market to make money. A scalper, a Japanese samurai, comes to the market to buy under his monthly support because it was the right thing to do. As it was the right thing to do, he did it.

So I can tell you that I scalp in 100 ticks, in Heikin Ashi on the Dax 30 and on the Dow Jones 30 with a five-minute chart to help me spot the trend, but that isn't worth much if you don't accept this scalping philosophy. You take your winnings quickly, you never let a winning trade turn into a losing trade. When you take 3 points and the price goes up +15 it's a great trade.

It took me years to accept this idea, this simple idea is really at the heart of scalping. You cash out your winnings quickly or you secure them with a TP +1 to try to make it a day trade.

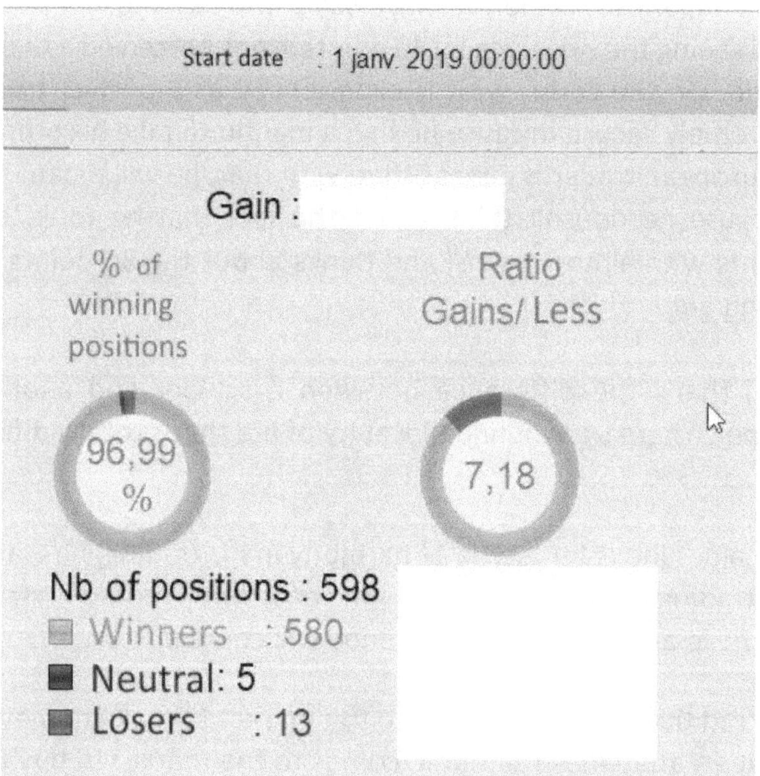

Trading results between 1st January 2019 and 10 May 2019, the date the digital manuscript was sent to the publisher

You have to completely rewrite your software. We, in Europe, are not used to thinking like that at all.

But, we manage to have a more than 90% success rate, a profit factor higher than 5, a magnificent equity curve.

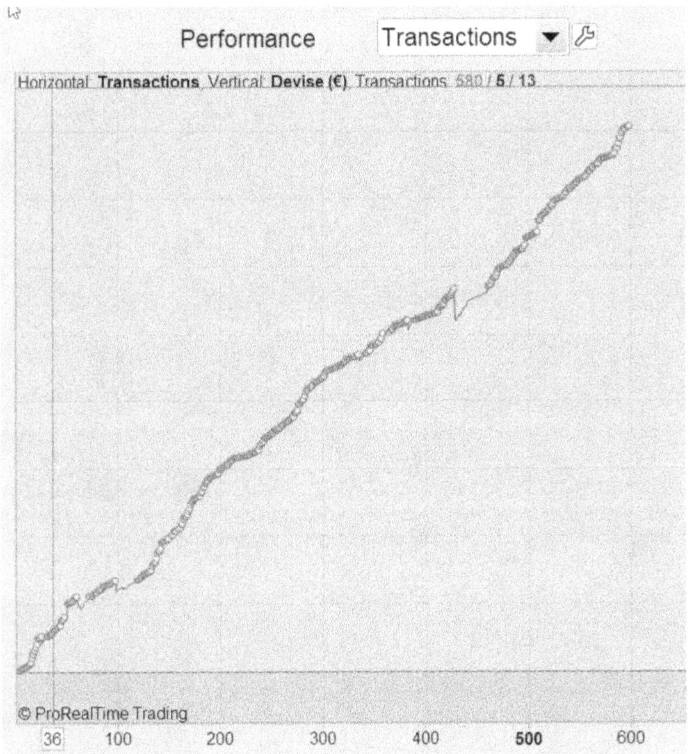

Scalping, there's really nothing complicated about it. We are constantly buying in the five-minutes trend and for 100 ticks. You wait, you wait for the prices to move and hit major supports and that's all scalping is. And to achieve this, we need to be incredibly disciplined, because everything in our education has to be rewritten. Scalping is, above all, a philosophy of life, a vision of trading and not a technique.

Because, even with the best technique in the world, if you feel frustrated taking 2 points when the price goes up by 15, you won't be able to make the distance. Your frustration will take over. You've gained 2 points, celebrate!

22

SCALPING SYMBOLIC LEVELS

I especially enjoy scalping symbolic levels. What I call symbolic levels are all levels 100, zones 250, 500, 750 and 1,000.

Example using the CAC 40, the symbolic levels are 4,000, 4,100, 4,200 4,250, 4,300, 4,400, 4,500, 4,600, 4,700, 4,750, 4,800, 4,900, 5,000.

Example using the Dow Jones 30, the symbolic levels are 25,000, 25,100, 25,200, 25,250, 25,300, 25,400, 25,500, 25,600, 25,700, 25,750, 25,800, 25,900, 26,000

I take these levels from cash. I find that cash levels are more effective for symbolic levels.

I prefer to see levels xx25 and xx75 as areas of indecision and avoid working on them.

The market often stagnates in these areas, wondering where to go. When it is in a xx25 zone, it hesitates to keep going up and reach xx50 or to go down to reach the hundred xx00.

I consider there to be a hierarchy of symbolic levels. Level 1,000 is the one that works best, followed by level 500, then 250 and finally every 100.

Like scalping Pivot Points, always buy under the support or over the resistance on the first pass of the day, aiming for re-integration.

If the price comes close or touches the level and rebounds, our transaction is not executed. You mustn't feel frustrated. We try to be like Japanese traders, making the perfect trade. We start a sort of quest for perfection and we can't be satisfied with buying over a support or on a support.

By being more exacting on our entries, we obviously have fewer trades, but they are of better quality.

It is important to remember that in a few minutes for scalpers, in a few hours for day traders and in a few days for swingers we will have totally forgotten the existence of this trade because we will have entered a lot of others.

When you feel frustration mounting, because your trade hasn't been executed, think about it: why get angry, why try to "chase the rabbit" and find yourself buying at a higher level (it's happened to all of us), when we're going to forget it even exists.

A case of scalping on a symbolic level

Take a textbook case, we're on the Dow Jones 30 at 26,200. When we get to the 26,000 level for the first time, we know it's an area that will be of interest to scalpers.

The question is when to open a position.

Exactly the same as for Pivot Points. You have to consider symbolic levels in the same way as you do Pivot Points.

There are, however, some specificities peculiar to each index. When you break a hundred for the first time in the day and with normal volatility:

On the Dax 30: a purchase around 90 for a resale around 95 can be profitable.

On the Dow Jones 30: a purchase around 75/80 for a resale around 90/92 can be profitable.

As you can see there are big differences between the Dax 30 and the Dow Jones 30.

Two things to note:

The first observation is that we must not forget that we are trying to reintegrate the symbolic level in the first pass.

Very often the trade moves towards the symbolic level and exceeds it. But by planning to resell it before it even reaches its symbolic level, we give ourselves a high probability of our trade succeeding.

The second observation is that I have integrated the difference in dynamics of each index. The Dow Jones 30 is more nervous than the Dax 30, so I try to get in on a 75/80 level, if my trade is executed, I have a very nice potential scalp.

If I try to get into the 90 on the Dow Jones 30, two out of three times I'm going to see it move towards level 75 before bouncing back. And if it moves towards level 75, since I entered at 90, I end up with minus 15. If it bounces off 75, I'm going to exit flat as a precaution.
All in all, I've gained nothing, I've put myself in a difficult situation and I've lost energy due to stress. I traded because I was afraid to miss out, because I was afraid to see it take off without me. It is, in fact, a disaster even if I didn't lose any money.

As you can see, even if the technique is the same, I don't behave at all the same way depending on the index used. That's why you have to spend hundreds, thousands of hours "eating your charts" so that you know your index intimately. We understand that we cannot spread ourselves too thinly by wanting to trade three indices, 10 stocks, three currencies, oil, gold and, because my neighbour told me it was good, Bitcoin. With experience, xx50 levels are also good for scalping, you can make some very lucrative trades under the strongest symbolic levels.

If the market descends, it is nervous and it reaches a very strong symbolic level like a 1,000 points zone (11,000 on the Dax 30, 23,000 on the Dow Jones 30 etc.) that it hasn't seen for a long time (you see that there are a lot of conditions) the possibility of moving back to 10,950 on the Dax 30, 22,950 on the Dow Jones 30 can make for a very nice day's trading. I find that, on the first break on the first pass of the 1,000 points zones, if they are pushed in a clean way, the algorithms try to save the support. Plus, it's a blessing for scalpers, day traders and swingers. So, there are a lot of people out there and, potentially, the possibility of a big bounce.

23

RANGE TRADING

I'm going to share with you a range technique that works well but only a few days a year because you need a particular context.

How to trade on a U.S. holiday on the European stock markets

My way of trading, on a holiday in the United States of America, when the European markets are open, assumes that European markets are not leaders, so they are not going to take any risks. Barring any exceptional economic news, they will remain within the known boundaries of the U.S. markets' closings the day before. The American markets are the leading markets, European managers and traders will therefore remain "wisely" in known zones, limited in advance, helped by algorithms.

Effectively, it would be "risky" for European managers and traders to take initiatives and to shift European indices too

too strongly up or down. It would be risky to anticipate the future American trend.

In general, and I repeat, barring exceptional events or special news, European markets tend to fall into this range as a precautionary measure.

Definition of range

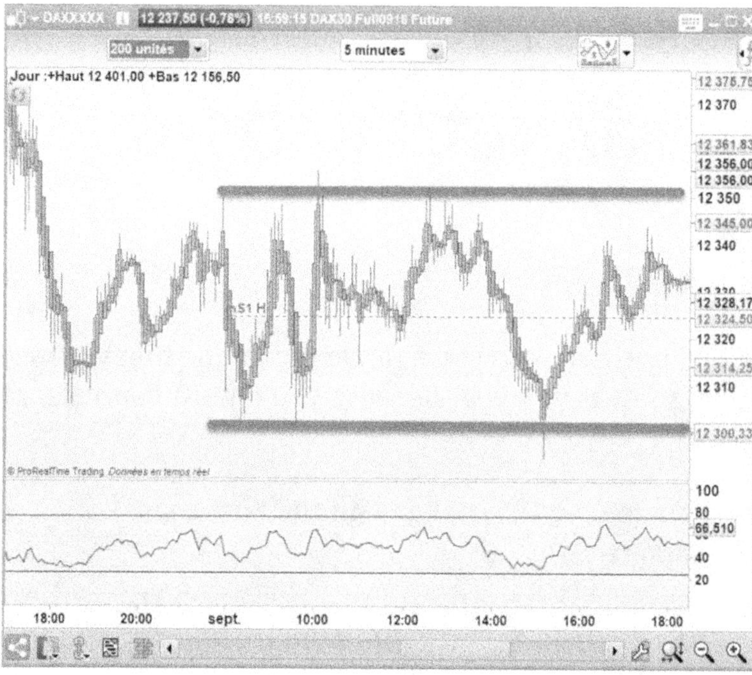

Date: Labour Day holiday in the United States of America and the DAX 30 price.

The range is defined by taking the lows and highs of the futures markets after the European markets close until 10 p.m., the closing time of the U.S. markets.

That gives us a working basis. Then you have to wait to check if these boundaries are validated, generally after the opening of the European markets at 9 a.m.

As you can see on this graph, the boundaries have been validated, so all we have to do is use them throughout the day on the basis that there is little risk of falling outside this range.

In this way I favour an entry on the second pass of the range (the first pass having limited the range by the definition of the high point and the low point). As soon as I see it bounce on 100 ticks I start to follow it until it breaks 5 minutes.

Depending on the market climate, if it's really calm, I'll try to take a third pass but much more cautiously. If we get close to the closing of the European markets, I won't take it.

However, I would like to stress one fact: if you are tired and in the interests of sound management of your efforts as a top-level sportsman, it would be better not to trade.

Effectively, this type of day involves tension related to monitoring the range's high and low points. Even if you set alarms, you'll think about it, you'll check it, etc. in short, you won't relax completely. You'll stay alert.

This type of day in the European markets when the U.S. stock exchanges are closed does not offer a huge potential for daily gains due to overwhelming volatility, but it is well secured especially if you follow the movement on the second pass.

It's up to you to judge whether it's worth it.

On the other hand, and this is extremely important, I will not do anything on the range's third contact for safety reasons. This is the moment when it could potentially break.

And you will understand why I am suspicious of the range's third contact, even during a holiday in the United States of America, when you study break trading.

24

BREAKOUT TRADING

I'm going to share a range technique that works very well in a market defined by a strong trend.

The idea is to identify the breakout possibilities which are very graphically characteristic.

When the market is trending (upwards or downwards), it encounters significant supports or resistances that prevent it from continuing its progress.

In these cases, the market does what I call 1, 2 and 3.

I test, I try, and I drill.

Let's take a closer look at this chart.

We're in a typical situation. The market has been bullish for several weeks now, and it is coming up on a fairly significant resistance as this is the weekly Pivot Point.

It will firstly come to test the weekly Pivot Point after 12 hours. The price is going down, sellers are active. It's just very typical, it is absolutely exceptional that you can free yourself of a weekly resistance on the first try. One hour later, the market starts moving again, this is the phase when it may break this resistance and move north.

But, I know that, statistically, it has a better chance of going back down. That's what it does. And, from that point on, I'm very focused because we have to monitor Dow's law. As you can see on the chart the low points are getting higher and higher.

Sellers are less active; prices don't fall much.

It's better for them to leverage the S1 J to get back on course. This is a very strong signal.

Put yourself in the sellers' shoes. They underwent a first assault that was brilliantly repulsed. They were attacked a second time and there they pushed their opponents back a little. And the buyers are back on the offensive.

You're a defender on your weekly Pivot. What would you do?

Faced with the desire of buyers, in an uptrend, there is only one thing left for hard sellers to do, retreat to regroup on the higher daily Pivot Point and abandon the weekly Pivot Point.

On the third pass, bingo. What I just described to you, I shared that live on the Andlil forum. I explained that there was a very good chance of a "bullish breakout".

You can find this type of configuration quite often when the market has a clear trend.

I told you about working with maps and observing to find your trading method. I found this technique one Sunday in the middle of my dozens of printed sheets. This market situation has become one of my favourites.

To remember for a maximum chance of getting a breakout

1) I test

2) I try

3) I drill

Now, I'm going to tell you my favourite technique, because it lets you maximize the gains while minimizing the risks.

Imagine, you're in the casino, you're playing roulette, you're betting on black and red comes out. You lost. But the casino spins the roulette wheel again to give you a chance to get your bet back. That the dream! In trading, we can almost do the same thing and that's what we're going to look at now.

25

TAKE YOUR LOSSES: MILITARY TECHNIQUE

One of the big problems for novice traders is knowing where to place their stops and I'm going to spend some time on this issue.

The first thing to remember is that you don't open a position without having estimated its possible loss. And it's not after entering the market that you start asking yourself the question nor when you start to make losses!

Before I even open a position, I first assess my possible loss based on the supports and resistances I see. One military technique I like to use to place my stops is what I call the second line of defence.

Think of your chart as a battlefield. You have real-time representation of the forces at work: buyers and sellers.

If your support is broken, if your first line is broken by enemy troops, your soldiers retreat to the second line of defence where they find reinforcements. During trench warfare in 1914-1918, there were successions of trenches like this, one after the other.

When the trenches in the first line seemed lost, the soldiers abandoned them and took refuge in the second trenches where they formed a resistance zone again. Very often with the troop reinforcements in the second trench, they began to attack again to retake the positions they had abandoned.

For me the financial markets work the same way. You have a front line where the price is created, and you have lines of defence (the SI S2 S3 supports) and lines of resistance (the R1 R2 R3 resistances).

The idea is that, before you enter the market, you need to check that you have support lines close and strong enough to help you come out flat if things go wrong. You must think like a soldier who is always in the middle of a fight and always knows where he must go if he is ordered to advance and/or surrender if he is ordered to retreat.

Let's take a case in point.

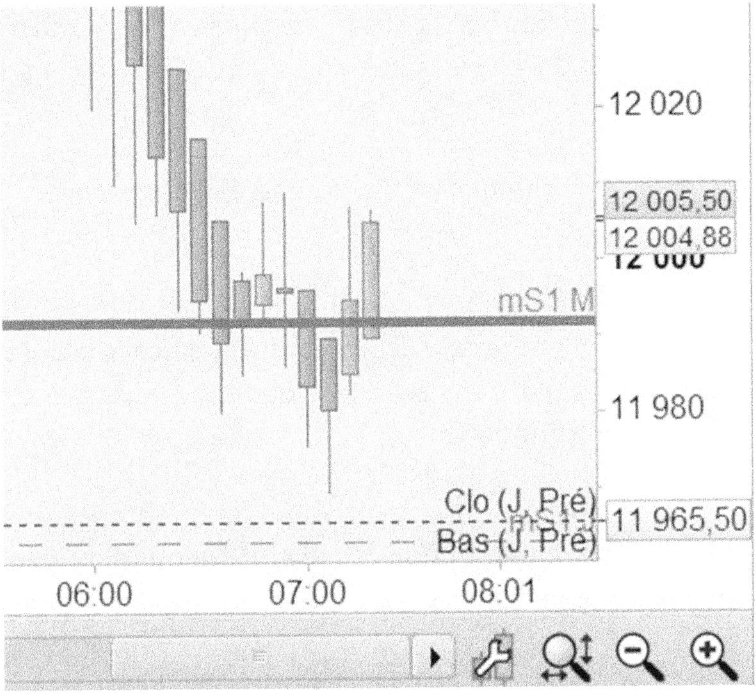

You decided to buy slightly under the mS1 M support of the Dax 30 during the first pass and, by buying under the support as we have seen, you had the possibility to make a scalping gain of 5 to 10 points.

But, too greedy, like a lot of novice scalpers, you wanted more. You didn't cash out your gains and the position went down. Bottom line, you're in trouble and in the red.

But fortunately, you have your second line of defence consisting of the previous day's lowest, the previous day's closing and an m S1 J.

The technique, on this type of configuration, is to put your stop loss under these 3 trenches, these 3 supports and to watch what happens there. If these 3 supports are breached again, your stop loss is triggered, and you take your losses.

But there is a high probability that the price will rebound from the previous day's close, allowing you to exit without any crushing damage.

It's the military technique of the double line of defence.

Let me recap:

Remember that, to benefit from your statistical advantage, you must always place the purchase under a support and the sale order over a support.

Your stop loss depends on the second line of defence which, if it goes wrong, gives a good chance of rebounding so that you can come out flat.

Effectively, it is very unlikely that a price will breach several supports in a straight line without a retracement (unless there is exceptional news).

By proceeding with this military logic, you increase your chances of gains if your trades are executed and if it goes wrong you increase your chances of coming out flat.

What if the second line of defence is too far away?

Sometimes the second line of defence is, for example, more than 40 points away.

If your money management does not allow you to cash in a loss of this intensity, you can look to see if there is a symbolic support. Symbolic supports work as well as Pivot Points.

If there is no second line of defence nearby, if you are in no-man's-land, the best thing to do is not to take a position.

If you enter the market you take a greater risk than usual because you don't have the safety net, the second line of defence that can come into play when you're in trouble.

That's why the best traders use these intellectual and somewhat military gymnastics. I only enter the market if my back is covered, if I have supports or significant symbolic levels behind me.

But let's start again because things have changed on the front lines.

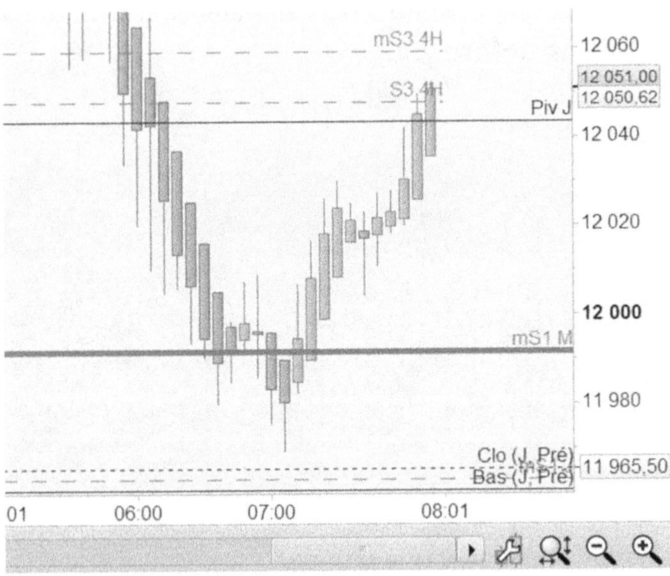

Your second line of defence has not been reached, your army attacks more effectively and the Bears seem to be retreating.

The military technique continues. You're going to put your second line of defence back in. For example, under m S1M, which will give you a small gain but let's you survive the course, or under Pivot J which gives you a nice gain but being close to the front, you risk being executed.

What I want to show you with these examples is that you must always be fluid and adapt yourself in trading. Better than that, you must always have this "attack-defence" state of mind, like a strategist, and always before going back in position ask yourself these questions:

Where is my second line of defence? (distance in points)
Is this distance suitable for my money management?
How strong is that second line? (Monthly or Daily support?)

Be strategic with your stock market positions and your results will increase considerably! The financial markets are a war-game unfolding before your eyes.

26

ON WHICH DAYS SHOULD TRADING BE AVOIDED?

Even if you are passionate about trading, you have to be rational. To remain efficient in long-term trading, you also need to allow yourself rest periods. If you trade every day of the year, you will lose efficiency, yield and risk near nervous or psychological exhaustion. Burnout is not far away.

For passionate traders, not trading for a day is like being punished. But we have to overcome this frustration and remember the basics: we are here to earn money as comfortably as possible. And for that, we need to take a break. No professional football player plays all the games of the season. The coach manages his team and rotates them.

You are your own coach and you must manage your team which consists of: YOU. You are the main capital of your trading company; you represent 100% of your human and intellectual capital. You must take care of yourself.

Have a coach's eye on yourself. A coach's objective, when doing this, is to get the best out of his player, to reveal and improve his potential (perhaps to sell him to the next Mercato). You are the cornerstone of your stock market results and possibly your trading company. Always keep a distance from your situation, constantly take a step back from your actions, activity, reactions and health.

Fortunately, there are some trading days that could be days off. Effectively, these days represent either an extremely high risk that should be avoided or a high probability that nothing will happen. And in that case, you will spend your day behind the screen for nothing, instead of rebuilding your psychological and mental capital for the next few days of competition.

Personally, I force myself not to trade on American holidays. I meant to say, "I force myself", because I experience it as a type of punishment. So, you have to find a way of not breaking down.

Why do I avoid trading on American holidays?

These types of days are generally completely dead in Europe. The European indices start to rank themselves in extremely narrow margins for hours. Remember that, for an index such as the CAC 40, 60% of the volume comes from the United States of America. So, when the American stock exchanges are closed, two things happen:

1) Volumes collapse and European indices have low volatility

2) Unless there is an absolutely extraordinary event, nothing generally happens

Objectively, for yield, it is not the type of day that will bring you the most money. You may end up in the green, but you will have lost a day of rest that would have enabled you to be more efficient in the following days. Moreover, if you are not patient by nature, you risk making that famous trade, out of boredom, that will ruin your week.

These are the main U.S. holidays on which the U.S. stock exchanges (New York and Chicago) are closed. There are nine days of forced rest per year, here is the list for the year 2019:

Tuesday, 1st January 2019: New Year's Day
Monday, 21st January 2019: Commemoration of Martin Luther King
Monday, 18th February 2019: President's Day
Friday 19 April 2019: Good Friday
Monday 27th May 2019: Memorial Day
Thursday, 4th July 2019: American Independence Day (half-day trading, closing at 1pm, French time)
Monday, 2nd September 2019: Labour Day
Thursday, 23rd November 2019: Thanksgiving (half-day trading, closing at 1pm, French time)
Wednesday, 25th December 2019: Christmas Day (half-day trading, closing at 1pm, French time)

Every two months, you have this space to be able to "breathe". And I insist, you have to really take a break, that is, not to trade of course, but also not to look at prices, not to work on charts, etc. Give yourself three days to take a break, to rest, to get out of the market completely, to enjoy your family, etc. If you trade on your own account, this is the ideal time to plan your long weekends, your short holidays, etc.

These periods should be seen as periods of absolute rest, allowing you to return to the financial markets in top form and lucidity. This may help you avoid a devastating burnout for your wallet. I've known hardcore traders who didn't take their fatigue into account. All in all, it ended badly, exhausted nervously, they all "tilted" one by one. No elite athlete competes every day. But a trader trades every day, it's a competition. So, you should think about taking it easy too.

For the year 2019, notice that Thanksgiving falls on a Thursday. You could also take Friday off, because American traders take the opportunity to take a day off. They usually spend a four-day weekend enjoying their family and shopping. So, Friday will be almost dead on the American stock exchange (and therefore in Europe).

What are the other trading periods to avoid during the year?

The last week of the year between Christmas and New Year's Day is, in my opinion, to be absolutely forbidden. It is usually a long, dull week with little volume and is punctuated by half-days of trading. And frankly, you have better things to do during this period than to collect a few points.

It is also the week of the year's results, of the good resolutions for next year (which will have to be kept), a week to calmly take stock of your trading with as much lucidity as possible. All the tension accumulated during the year is slowly lowered.

I'll go even further. Personally, I stop trading for the last two weeks of the year. I find that the week before Christmas is often "dicey". I consider that in the year we have 50 weeks of trading and that the last two weeks of the year are dead weeks for trading.

Of course, we usually reach the end of the year tired, we lack clarity. But also, some managers take the opportunity to liquidate positions to consolidate their annual results.

And I have a traumatic memory from the 2000s, when I was a teacher, of having destroyed a wonderful year of trading in the last two weeks of the year.

So now, distrusting myself all the time, it's two weeks off the market. I calmly prepare for my new trading year, I assess my progress, my statistics, I reread my trading journal for the year to revive my acquired experience, work on setting up charts that I think I will track. We slowly release the tension, the stress of the year as we prepare for resurgence.

A trader, like Janus, must always look back to the past to gain experience and look to the future to improve.

Why don't I trade when there are ECB and FOMC announcements?

I also do not trade on ECB and FOMC announcement days. Indeed, I find these days particularly dangerous.

Before the central banks' monetary decisions are announced, the order books gradually empty. All market professionals withdraw and take a step back. This, of course, is when all novice traders rush to trade.
Their excitement can be felt, it is palpable on the stock market forums. They know that fat candles are possible, a high probability of volatility and that attracts them. It's stronger than they are, no matter how much they are warned, they still open positions and they are often in tears at the end of the day.

They have neither the experience to navigate during a storm nor the capital to withstand strong intraday variations that may occur. And yet, we are fortunate to know this potential danger.

We survive on the stock market by dodging bullets, not by rushing to meet them. When the weather forecast announces a hurricane risk, we do not see boaters rushing out to sea to experience the sensations. They calmly stand by watching the storm in the distance.

So, these are the times of the year when I don't trade. This enables me to rest and avoid the potentially most dangerous trading days. The main objective, of a trader on his own account, is to be consistent and avoid significant capital losses.

But there is also a rhythm during the scholarship week and the special case of Friday that deserves to be studied.

27

WHY FRIDAY IS SPECIAL ON THE STOCK MARKET

Why do we tend to lose money in the stock market on Fridays rather than on other days? You must have thought this at some time: "but why did I just lose my week in the financial markets on the last trades on Friday? "

Trader fatigue

Let's face it, trading is extremely stressful. It's not a physical job, you sit on a chair all day long, it's not a very intellectual job, when you have good command of your trading, you just have to wait.

But it's very stressful. And little by little, we lose our effectiveness. So, we very often get to Fridays less lucid than the previous days. Fatigue also leads to less self-control and therefore less analysis and placing trades that are often less relevant.

Friday is a special time on the financial markets

Friday is not a typical day in the financial markets. Effectively with the weekend, many Hedge Funds decide not to take any risk and have to liquidate their positions.

That's why there is a lot more nervousness generally at the close of the European markets on Fridays and even more so at the close of the US markets.

So, we are tired after a week of trading when the market can become potentially the most volatile and dangerous.

Fear of missing trades

If you're a passionate trader like me, there's a good chance you'll lose some of your winnings on Fridays because subconsciously you're starting to get anxious. Effectively, the weekend is coming up.

And at weekends, you have to be happy, it's a social obligation: you have to go to restaurants, you have to go to museums or cinemas, you have to practice sports, you have to go shopping and wander around to see the consumer society.

But if you're a trading addict like me, that is incredibly boring. The only interesting thing, which doesn't happen at the weekend, is the opening of the financial markets. So, we just have to be patient and think about Monday, when real, exciting life begins again.

So psychologically, unconsciously, we tend to cut ourselves off on Fridays so that we can brood all weekend. That way, we are constantly on the financial markets, we spend the whole weekend thinking, pondering, being in a rather gloomy mood with those around us.

But in the end, unconsciously, that was what we were looking for when we were getting the Friday hit. Intellectually we stay in the financial markets all weekend, just brooding, brooding, brooding.

How to trade well on a Friday in the financial markets

In conclusion, we must take these three factors into account for this very special day, Friday.

Consider our tiredness, take into account that Friday can be much more volatile and take into consideration our passion and the fact that we are starting to worry about a very long weekend without trading.

Going beyond that
Once you have mastered your trading, there are some nice moves to try sometimes on US indices after the European close. If the market is in a very strong and clear trend, for example, the trend is bullish all week without running out of steam, you can close on a weekly high at the Wall Street close. The market is generally soft and the Dow Jones 30 progresses slowly but with a regularity typical of algorithms. If it's been a good week, you may want to take the risk of sacrificing a few points to attempt a long, slow upward climb until 10 pm. With experience, you can identify this type of market. Of course, it doesn't work every time, it requires good entry timing, but when it works it's great to leave the markets on a Friday night on the highest point of the week. Of course, this is recommended for more experienced traders and only if you want to sacrifice a Friday night monitoring your position.

28

EVALUATING TRADING QUALITY

Now that you have defined your intervention strategy, identified the days to avoid and mastered your trading method, you will have to evaluate it as honestly as possible.

There are two indicators to evaluate the quality of your trading which are relentless: Profit Factor and Maximum Drawdown.

Evaluating your performance is essential to adapting your strategy to the market. Indeed, as we have already mentioned, a strict and non-evolving trading method has an extremely limited lifespan. Financial markets are evolving and changing all the time. In fact, we are experiencing an acceleration of cycles in finance. Until a few decades ago, a method could last five or six years and be cost-effective. Now, if it lasts 18 months without any change, it's very noteworthy.

Your trading method must, therefore, adapt and constantly evolve with the market. The Holy Grail of miracle methods, operating on multi-markets for the next 20 years, is a child's dream.

Note that you also will be constantly evolving. You won't be the same psychologically at all five years from now. Well, I hope not, because the market won't have waited for you to change.

The path you have taken as a trader is one of searching, perseverance and constant suffering. That's also the beauty of this job, you have to constantly question yourself. Certainly, in five years, I'll be trading differently. I may have changed instruments, because the Dax 30 or the Dow Jones 30 has evolved and I don't appreciate its new volatility, for example.

But like any change, with our noses to the grindstone, or rather in our charts, we don't necessarily perceive it quickly. But if your Profit Factor or Maximum Drawdown suddenly changes, it should be seen as a warning. Maybe something is going on. Is the market changing? But perhaps it is you who has changed, who without realizing it is no longer concentrating as much as before for X reason and introspection is valuable and necessary in that case.

The Profit Factor and Maximum Drawdown are, therefore, not only indicators for evaluating the quality of your trading but also leading indicators of a change or evolution that must be closely monitored to remain effective. Because your method will evolve for two main reasons. Financial markets are constantly changing and so are you. By embarking on the path of trading, you will inevitably evolve, progress most likely, doubt certainly. Trading is a great mirror of the self. It doesn't forgive anything, but it's always just like the Profit Factor and Maximum Drawdown. It's real, nothing but real.

Definition of Profit Factor

Profit Factor is an index of trading skills. It gives a figure which evaluates the ratio between the risks taken and your trading results.

If your trading is good, your Profit Factor will be higher than 2. Below this figure, you need to review your trading, even if you are making profits.

A Profit Factor of less than 2 shows that the risks taken to increase your capital are too high. In the medium term, a trader with a Profit Factor of less than 2 is statistically doomed, the risks being too high to make a profit. This means that, at some point, losses will take the lead and you cannot recover. With a Profit Factor greater than 2, your losses are covered.

How is Profit Factor calculated?

Profit Factor is calculated very simply: you add up all your winning trades and divide them by all your losing trades:

Profit Factor = (sum of earnings) / (sum of losses)

Profit Factor: practical example

For example, on a trading day, all your winning trades come to €530, your total losses €280. At the end of the day, you have made €250 net and your Profit Factor is: 1.89 (530/280=1.89).

So, your day is positive, you are happy to have made a PV of €250. However, the lower than 2 Profit Factor should warn you: you have taken too high a risk to make this amount, you tangibly lost €1 to earn €1.89. In the long term, your trading is too dangerous. Of course, for one day that holds little value, you must assess Profit Factor weekly, monthly, quarterly, and annually. The longer the period the calculation is based on, the more relevant the result is and the more it qualitatively characterises your trading.

Profit Factor and risk management

Profit Factor is, therefore, a powerful risk management tool that is often used by Hedge Funds to assess traders. The general philosophy of these Hedge Funds is a high yield with minimum risk. We need to adopt this philosophy in our personal trading: so, it is better to make an average of €200 per day, with a Profit Factor of 3 (making an average of €300 for every €100 loss) than €400 per day with a Profit Factor of 2 (making €200 on average for every €100 loss)!!!

My approach to Profit Factor

This tool is often used by American Hedge Funds because it is relentless, you know immediately if the profits have been generated soundly and securely or unconsciously.

In France, it is virtually unheard of, although it should be mandatory in deciding where to place money in the various funds. Yield is not everything, the security of the placement is the first condition to be taken into consideration.

For my trading, I calculate my Profit Factor every week, every month, and every year as you can see in my stock market results.

This enables me to assess my trading skills over time, to try to improve each day, week, month, year. Also, I prefer to make €3,000 a week with a Profit Factor of 7 than €5,000 with a Profit Factor of 3. If you want to evaluate traders' skills, ask for their Profit Factor. If they do not know what it is, they are not a trader but a clown.

Maximum Drawdown

Maximum Drawdown, or Max Drawdown for short, is an indicator of trading quality and risk management.

To improve your trading, you need to know how to analyse the quality of your trading. The Profit Factor coupled with Maximum Drawdown will give you a statistical, "honest" view of your trading quality.

Of course, you have to put this in perspective with your goals and your psychological feelings.

You can make money, have good Drawdown and Profit Factor and yet know that you traded badly because you used too much leverage, that you almost cracked, etc. things these indicators won't be able to tell you, only you can truly 'feel' your trading.

Definition of Maximum Drawdown

Maximum Drawdown indicates the historical maximum loss that an unlucky investor would have suffered if he had bought at the high and sold at the low for a specified period.

It is one of the instruments used by Hedge Funds to evaluate traders.

If a trader makes money but has a Max Drawdown of -20% for example, he will find himself out the door.

How to calculate Max Drawdown

It's very simple, you have to identify your maximum loss over a day, a week, a month, a year, etc.

Practical examples of Max Drawdown

Example 1, 4 trades in a day or week, it doesn't matter:

Trade 1: €+500
Trade 2: €-210
Trade 3: €+50
Trade 4: €+150

Simple, your Maximum Drawdown is €-210.

If you have €10,000 capital, you can calculate it by % (210/10,000) *100=2.1.

Your Max Drawdown for the day is -2.1% of your capital.

Example 2, 8 trades and it gets complicated:
Trade 1: €+120
Trade 2: €+300
Trade 3: €-330
Trade 4: €+50
Trade 5: €-100
Trade 6: €+200
Trade 7: €+350
Trade 8: €-250

What's the Maximum Drawdown?

€-330? You lost. It's €-380.
Maximum Drawdown is the historical maximum loss, not the trade that generated the most loss (nuance).

So, in this example in trade 3 we have €-330 Max Drawdown, Drawdown

Trade 4 at €+50 gives us a €-280 Drawdown (it's not the max anymore) (-330+50=280)

Then we can see €-100 with trade 5, which makes Max Drawdown of €-380 (-280-100=-380)

The €-330 Max Drawdown is a thing of the past, trade 6 at €+200 give us a Drawdown (not maximum) of €-180, the 7th trade of €+350 gives us a Drawdown of 0 (-180+500=320) because the Drawdown base is zero and can only be negative.

The last trade at €-250 makes a Drawdown €-250 which can become max if the next trade, 9, is €-150 for example (-250-150=-400).

Profit Factor and risk management

So Maximum Drawdown is a little perverse. You can't avoid it; you can make 50 winning trades and it's there waiting for you at the turn.

If you chain bad trades together, they accumulate, and Maximum Drawdown keeps increasing but can never be reabsorbed.

My vision of Max Drawdown

Maximum Drawdown is, therefore, an instrument to determine the quality of an investment, a formidable complement to the Profit Factor.

Of course, no investment fund highlights their Maximum Drawdown, we would be very surprised.

So, we can post 51% growth on a financial product. But if it has a Max Drawdown of -17%, if you are unlucky and buy it at the highest you can lose 17% too. (And if the future is the same as the past of course, which does not happen).

On the other hand, an investment at +15% with a Max Drawdown of -2% is much more attractive, you risk -2% at most to gain +15% at most.

Using the Profit Factor and Maximum Drawdown together gives you an honest look at your trading activity and accurate knowledge of the risks you are taking.

It's time to question yourself.

29

ANNUITY OR ACCUMULATION TRADING

Accumulation trading is the most common type of trading. It consists of making your capital grow because there is not enough of it to do annuity trading. This is generally a more aggressive form of trading, sometimes using high leverage.

Effectively, the small initial amount often leads to a lot of frustration. Real earnings are low due to the lack of capital. Generally, after a while, there is the temptation to increase the speed, to increase leverage to accelerate things. But low leverage or high leverage trading is like driving at 90 km/h or 300 km/h. It is not at all the same thing and many traders end up going to the wall as a result of uncontrolled leverage slippage.

I spent more than 10 years doing accumulation trading. I wasted many years trying to move too fast. This is the most frustrating type of trading ever. We often have the impression that we are not moving fast enough, and we want to speed things up. It's a little like the fable of the hare and the tortoise. It's important to try to stay consistent, even if it's frustrating. If I had stayed constantly with the tortoise's viewpoint, I would have achieved annuity trading much faster than I did with my hare’s viewpoint. Only regularity in trading pays off in the medium and long term.

Trading is the most frustrating activity I have ever practised. Traders are never satisfied, even when they have had a good trade. A few minutes later, they could be disappointed because they exited too early. That's why the best traders are the ones who can handle frustration. And for that, you have to do a great deal of psychological work on yourself. The key to success is not in the trading method, in the technique. That's a small part of the trader's equation.

It's personal psychology that's paramount. Actually, managing permanent frustration should be at the centre because we are very exposed to it with accumulation trading. I think that the main objective of accumulation trading should be to be able to obtain a sum comfortable enough to switch to the more pleasant trading, annuity trading and not "to get rich".

Annuity trading is the most psychologically pleasing trading because it consists of managing your capital with due diligence. The capital amount must be sufficient to generate an annuity that enables you to live according to your personal criteria.

Some people can live very comfortably on €2,000 per month and others find it difficult to make ends meet on €20,000 per month. The capital can, therefore, be very variable depending on the trader, a flashy trader and a humbler trader do not have the same needs at all.

There is much less aggression in annuity trading. Ideally, you should be able to trade under leverage and not exceed leverage of 2. This is a really comfortable trading zone. The degree of comfort will, of course, go hand in hand with the amount of initial capital. If I need €2,000 per month net to live, it will be much easier psychologically to achieve it with €1,000,000 on my trading account than with €100,000. The more money we have in the stock market, the easier it is to earn it because there is less pressure.

Also, we tend to trade much less. When you trade regularly, you set yourself monthly objectives. When they are reached, we tend to slow down for the rest of the month. Effectively, the job is done so we tend to watch the stock market to take advantage of very good opportunities. We no longer have to look to the markets for a few crumbs. This is what many accumulation traders do not understand.

For example, I am often asked about the fact that I could trade with a lot more lots. That's what I would have done if I was doing accumulation trading. But with my annuity trading, my goal is first and foremost to generate income with minimum risk and therefore minimum stress. Above all, I practice conservation trading. I have absolutely no further need to take risks. If you trade prudently and reasonably, you reach your goal at the end of the month without any stress peaks.

It should be pointed out that annuity trading is easier at the moment because you don't have to chase after inflation. In an inflationary period, annuity trading is more complicated. Effectively, you have to be able to feed yourself and also increase your capital by the value of inflation so that you don't find yourself in difficulty after 10 to 20 years with capital that is no longer worth anything.

Inflation is the enemy of annuity trading; it gradually eats away at capital. For example, before the First World War, France had a large number of pensioners. They were ruined by post-war inflation, which sometimes rose to more than 20% per year. Annuity trading is therefore ideal in times of deflation or low inflation. And if inflation comes back, you have to go back to slightly more aggressive trading to accumulate to compensate for the inflationary effect (you can also hedge against inflation quite easily, something our ancestors couldn't do). Therefore, annuity trading is not a panacea either. Inflation must be closely monitored. Recent years, with the crisis, have been bread and butter for annuity traders, but how long will this last?
As you will have understood, accumulation trading and annuity trading are two opposite trading styles.

With accumulation trading, there is a tendency to take risks, to use leverage. So, there is a tendency to try "hits". At the end of the day, a lot of us are trying to get "rich", that's the underlying idea of an accumulation trader.

With annuity trading, we try to take as little risk as possible. We try not to use leverage and we have time on our hands. We have estimated that our capital is sufficient to live according to our standards. Accumulation only serves to enrich the State or our ungrateful heirs upon our death (humour).

So, I invite you to think about your type of trading, are you an annuity trader or an accumulation trader?

Do you want to become a proprietary trader to get rich or for quality of life?

And what capital do you need to aim for to become an annuity trader, if that's what you want?

You then have to estimate your real needs and, sometimes, totally question your way of life. You have a choice to make that will have serious consequences on your money management.

To think about
Accumulation trading is trading that necessarily uses high leverage to increase trading capital which has been deemed insufficient. I encourage you not to make the same mistake I made, which made me waste many years, wanting to go faster than the music. Take a few more years to build up your trading capital, you can profit in the medium term, time, quality of life, quality of trading, etc. In the end, isn't the ultimate goal of a trader to move towards annuity trading? Annuity trading enables you to gradually reduce the amount of leverage and improve the quality of trading, which becomes less stressful. Reducing trading stress, doesn't that sound great?

MY MONEY MANAGEMENT, RULES AND RITUALS

Persevere

30

CREATING THE FRAMEWORK

After a lot of research, you find a personal method that seems to work. To maintain it and give it a chance to succeed, you must determine your Money Management criteria, which is essentially based on your position size, optimal leverage and tolerated risk of loss per position.

You'll also need to identify your strengths. Your trading rules should optimize your strengths, protecting you from your negative impulses. This is an essential step in your Money Management and the development of your trading rules.

Your Money Management and trading rules are there as a framework and to guarantee the intervention strategy, your method on the financial markets that you have previously defined. These rules are set in stone.

You will also have to think about your daily ritual as a trader, how will you trade, under what conditions, for how long? This ritual will be there to secure you as you have secured your trading station.

It is forbidden and unthinkable to deviate from your own rules and laws. We will see in the next chapter, devoted to psychology, that it is not always easy to abide by your rules.

It is, therefore, necessary to work on a third stratum, your own psychology and emotional control, which in turn will make it possible to guarantee the application of Money Management and trading rules that themselves frame the intervention strategy and trading method.

But for now, you must define your framework, your trading ritual, the rules that frame your activity, protect it and allow it to flourish.

Things to remember
We have three layers like an onion, each covering the other: At the centre, at the heart, is the intervention strategy or trading method. This is encompassed and guaranteed by trading rules and Money Management. These are themselves encompassed and guaranteed by the mastery of your emotions and psychology. When these three layers cohabit perfectly together, you are an exceptional trader.

Let's recap
You're at stage two, a very difficult stage, it's the mirror stage, the perseverance stage. You need to ask yourself these questions over and over again to protect your trading method from yourself What are your strengths? What are your weaknesses? What is preventing you from perfectly implementing your trading method? What personal trading and Money Management rules are you going to put in place to increase your strengths and reduce your weaknesses and enable you to apply your trading method? This step can take several weeks, months (or years) to complete. It depends on how clear headed you are, on your ego... on perfection. The deeper you dig within yourself to discover yourself, the more you're going to see new problems, but also new strengths arise. You have to readjust your trading rules each time until you find a balance between yourself and your own rules. They will no longer be a constraint but a need, an obviousness that enables you to be serene in your trading, that gives you internal calm. You have to persevere, persevere, dig deeper and deeper into yourself to succeed in defining your own

safety rules to preserve your capital from a tilt, an accident, a crash that is caused only by yourself.

You have only one enemy in trading, and that's yourself. Protect yourself from yourself, now is the time to start.

31

MONEY MANAGEMENT, THE ART OF SURVIVAL

Trading and earning **money**, is good, trading while limiting losses, is better. That is the objective of Money Management.

Definition of Money Management

Money Management is the art of managing capital by applying tight capital risk management.

It is the most important element in trading after trading psychology, but novice traders often neglect it and only focus on gains and **technical analysis**.

However, to survive in the financial markets, and it is a war, you against other traders as trading is a zero-sum game, you must, above all, know yourself and know how to manage your capital. You'll find out later that this war is mostly between you and yourself.

Money Management is, therefore, rules and techniques that you must impose on yourself to succeed in trading. These should frame you and your trading method. By searching again and again you have managed to create your own trading method. It works but now you need to calibrate it, to limit it to fit your capital and your ambitions.

Money Management or the art of pessimism

Your capital is the determining element of your trading, it is your stock in trade. The more you have, the more possibilities you have to develop, the more you can spread out risks, like a business.

Your capital should be considered in the same way as business capital, each Euro is valuable. I am always surprised to hear people grumble because a loaf of bread has gone up in price by 10 cents, but then manage their capital without even considering the risks they take.

Before opening a position, the first question to ask yourself is: "what risks am I taking with my capital?" rather than "what are my profits going to be?" ". Always be pessimistic about your potential losses.

Personally, I evaluate, for example, a swing position in this way:

I evaluate swing positions in this way: If I open the position and the index loses -20% in the next few hours, what will my situation be?

If I can I survive. I open the position.

If I can't recover from it, I don't open the position, or I decrease **leverage**. Of course, you can place stop orders. But remember one thing, stop orders are not guaranteed. If certain events take place, your stop order could easily be executed 3% lower. You were leveraged 10:1? Ouch, -30% in 5 seconds.

Money Management is essential to surviving the financial markets

The financial markets are very unforgiving of any mistakes. You can earn money for years and lose everything in 20 seconds if you use too much leverage or if you do not have guaranteed stop orders... 10 years ago the attacks in the USA, flash crashes (some shares lost 90% in value in 5 minutes), massive sales of Dax futures by Société Générale, destabilising the price of futures (the Kerviel effect), one trader who drove the financial markets to collapse by passing a sell order for1 billion instead of one million (I have always been sceptical of this explanation). Each of these events had the potential to ruin you in a moment. If we note all of these major events, you will see that, on average, there is a major risk in the financial markets every 18 months. Your life expectancy is therefore statistically 18 to 24 months in the financial markets if you're not careful. If you're lucky, you survive the first ball, but watch out for the next ball!

I want to trade my capital for the next 50 years; therefore, I apply a very stringent Money Management strategy to protect my capital. Not losing money is more important for me than earning it.

The whole world can earn money, you can simply browse the broker forums, it is always possible to read about the exploits of some traders who are 200% up on the week. Bravo, but 2 weeks or 2 months later, there is no trace of this trader. This is not because he has become a billionaire, but he's had a bad day and has been levelled out. You are there for the long haul, not a fast burnout.

Different Money Management strategies

You must adapt your Money Management strategy to your capital. The simplest way is to set a capital loss limit. Personally, I set a daily loss limit in Euros. If I reach this limit, I stop trading. It is a simple Money Management strategy but is the most effective as it allows you to fully control your losses, no bad surprises.

The idea of this Money Management strategy is to accept a specified loss which will not jeopardise your capital. You can then restore your capital quickly, you don't risk vanishing into thin air, and you assume full control of the situation, you don't suffer more losses.

Of course, it is very hard to take losses, we prefer to let things run and wait, sometimes hoping for a miracle. This may work a few times but one day, just the once, the loss will be multiplied by X and you will be left with nothing. God must be a communist, he never intervenes to save traders.

The maximum loss I allow myself is double my daily earnings objective. If I lose one day, I must be able to recover the loss in 1 or 2 days. By the end of 3 days, say a week at the worst, my capital is replenished.

So, I only wasted time, not money. Of course, for this to work, you must have a success rate of close to 66%.

But the most important idea, in my opinion, is this:

The thing we worry about most in trading is a loss. By setting yourself a maximum daily loss, you are turning the problem around. You get up in the morning and you already know, at worst, what's going to happen. Then why the anguish? Loss is no longer your sneaky, unknown enemy. You just tamed it!

The limits of Money Management for small investors

Sometimes you read that you should only risk 1% of your capital per trade. In an ideal world, yes, that would be perfect because there is little chance that you could have 100 negative trades in succession. But this management strategy is useful for Hedge Funds which have significant capital and extremely low costs. If you have €10,000 to invest, taking every €100 loss is virtually impossible with the costs, minimum lot size, etc. If you have €1,000,000 to invest, a €10,000 loss is completely controllable.

This is, therefore, the paradox of Money Management in the financial markets, the more capital you have, the more efficient your Money Management strategy is, if you are sensible.

If you have modest capital, with a tight Money Management strategy, it will be more difficult to earn money because your stop orders are tighter and are triggered more often.

It can be summarized as follows: The more money you have, the easier it is to make more while taking little risk. The less money you have, the more difficult it is to make more as the risks are greater even with a good Money Management strategy.

Money Management conclusion

You must find a Money Management system adapted to your capital. You must always expect the worst because you will see the worst one day or another. On that day, there will be those who will never bounce back and those who will withstand it without flinching and be able to start again. The choice is yours.

My words may be a little harsh, but that is the principle of reality. "Life's unfair, I'm starting out, I have little capital and it's harder for me, etc." Yes, that's how it is, we all started that way. Have a good laugh and put yourself in action, but let it be a stimulus, a challenge.

And now that your trading method is secured by precise Money Management allowing you to limit your losses, we're going to look at the trading rules that will be engraved into the marble of your laws.

32

THE TRADER'S MANTRA

I am going to share my 7 trading rules with you. I read them each time I am going to trade. These are my mantras in a literal sense, my ritual step to put me in the right psychological state for trading and to simply check during the day if I am still capable of trading.

The term mantra, in Sanskrit, means tools of the spirit (Manas) and the suffix, 'tra', protection, from where the commonly accepted definition, protection of the spirit derives.

I use it to protect my own capital because I think that the greatest weakness for a trader, whether beginner or experienced (who, theoretically, is a master of his technique, his Money Management, his indicators, etc.) is himself.

We always come back to the essential point, how to manage stress, tension, how to stay clear-headed while trading. Of course, I analyse price curves throughout the day as well as changes in my emotional state. If any one of these rules is no longer upheld, I stop trading, it's the end of the day.

Trading rules are like a safeguard to compensate for your weaknesses and increase your strengths.

Strict application of these trading principles has transformed my results. These rules are not exceptional nor very original but since I started applying them to the letter my results are much more regular and consistent in terms of earnings.

The objective is not to suggest a single framework which can be applied to every trader, we are all individuals with our own psychological reactions and personal relationship with money, personal capital, etc.

These rules are adapted to my personality, my trading problems, my financial standing, etc. These are the psychological and technical techniques that I have put in place in trying to find solutions to overcome my weaknesses, to avoid repeating the same mistakes, etc. and make it into the 10% of traders who regularly earn on the financial markets.

Adapt your own rules to your trading style and personality only you can do this job, only you know yourself.
I will describe my trading rules in detail to help you. You may find some rules that apply to you, others you might find absurd, but they can give you ideas, paths to creating your own rules, your personal commandments.

You understand, of course, that it would be absolutely ridiculous to adopt my trading rules like this, they are the result of solving my personal problems, to apply my trading method.

It is above all a difficult thought process because you will have to really look in the mirror, without avoiding what you are, list all your mistakes and recurring weaknesses, find a way to get around them if you can't improve them.

A real thorough job awaits you:

Acknowledge, list and accept your weaknesses.

See how you can accommodate them within your trading to minimize their negative impact on your bottom line.

But you will also have to identify your strengths in trading, and you have them. Your trading rules will also need to optimize your strengths.

Back to work!

33

RULE NUMBER 1 DON'T LOSE ANY MONEY

It often makes people smile when I tell them that my number 1 rule is not to lose money on the financial markets. On my blog's financial markets forum, I often hear from traders who are dissatisfied at the end of the day because they have only earned a few euros whereas "if... ". I usually reply: "A day without loss is a good day". It may seem simplistic, but I became a winner by reversing my priority in the financial markets.

There are more losses than gains on the financial markets

I used to trade on the financial markets to earn money, a purchase was planned to gain, and a loss was, more or less, calculated. I was all-powerful, I was looking for a quick, easy profit, I didn't think much about possible losses because I was convinced of my analysis.

Now, I do (am) the opposite, I live in a state of perpetual doubt, I am no longer certain about the market's direction (the market has put me in my place often enough to teach me that certainty on the financial markets is a vote for major set-backs). Therefore, I calculate any possible loss first, I always take the most pessimistic position possible, I consider loss as a fact and profit as a possibility.

Trading is not a game

By proceeding like this your whole view of trading changes: trading is no longer a game, it becomes a risk. Your positions are then mechanically much more secure because you are trading from the viewpoint of risk reduction. Your trading will be "cleaner" and more efficient, less enjoyable certainly, but you must realize that you are trading to make money and not to have feelings. (broad topic).

Imagine the worst in trading

From the moment you are in this state of mind, permanent doubt will always make you imagine the worst-case scenario; the black days that plunge your annual results are greatly re-duced and you can avoid them. In my case, I had 5 or 6 days a year which wiped out my earnings; weeks of work reduced to nothing, sometimes in a few hours. This first rule, the golden rule, " Do not lose money" enables me to limit or even to erad-icate the black days to a large extent. I urge you to apply this principle to your last few trading years.

Find those black days or trades, analyse them and find a solu-tion to try to reduce them. In my case, it was my oversized ego: I was right, my analysis was correct, the market will prove me right when the stakeholders think about it. So, I doubled, tripled my positions, destructive pyramiding, etc. as if my modest lots had the slightest impact.

I did not want to accept my weakness, the fact that I am nothing in the financial markets, that what I think is of no consequence and that, ultimately, the financial markets is not about being right or wrong; it is just about trying to take advantage of a flow you can never control.

A day without loss is a good day on the financial markets

A day without loss is a wonderful day on the financial markets, capital is maintained, you have tried things, you have gained experience... and you are fully operational for the next day. And the profit? As Lacan said, it comes as a bonus, the priority is not to lose, to win in the end.

34

RULE NUMBER 2 REREAD RULE NUMBER 1

While Trading rule number 1 is not to lose money, trading rule number 2 is to: reread rule number 1.

You may find this trading rule funny or uninteresting, yet it is at the heart of any trading system: you must adhere to the rules that have been set if you want to make money in the long term, and this is certainly one of the hardest things for a trader to do.

I see it every day on my financial markets' forum, losing traders are always those who do not follow their own rules. Trading is a system of high probability, for its success rate to be consistent, you must apply the same rules continuously, it is by breaking these rules just once, by not respecting your

Money Management, that your financial markets results can collapse.

There are numerous psychological explanations which explain why traders regularly break their own trading rules, each trader should have a personal analysis, but we can draw up two fairly classic types of trader:

The casino trader or the pathological gambler

This is the type of trader that you most often meet, it is this type that has the least chance of surviving in the field of trading. He finds it impossible to follow the first rule, do not lose money, because he is essentially trading for the thrill. He is the prototype, classical casino player who is more concerned with the emotions and the dream than a return on his portfolio. His profits always seem inadequate to him, compared to his objectives.

He is a trader who is continually frustrated with his results and always wants more. If he succeeds in trading, he will take more and more risks, not to achieve his objectives but to increase his emotions, his tension. This personality always seeks out limits and constantly tries to stretch them. I knew a trader whose goal was to make 1 million euros, something he managed to achieve.

Once he achieved this objective, he found that one million euros was not enough, and he increased his goal to 2 million then five million euros. Always more, until his eventual downfall, until everything was lost, and he had to start again.

The pathological player does not aim to win, but often has an urge to repeat, he wins, he loses everything, he starts all over again.

Subconsciously, he is looking for the fall to be reborn; it is a way to feel alive, and to fight the fear of death: these are players who are constantly repeating the same mistakes because this repetition is reassuring and has the possibility of "renewal", to rise again like a phoenix.

The blinkered or egotistic trader

This is a well-known class of trader who bitterly haunts financial market forums. They are generally the most aggressive. These are traders, often with personalities filled with certainty, who can hardly develop. They assume, for example, that the market will collapse, and they believe this at all costs. Their choice is made; nothing can move them, even reality.

Therefore, they are not able to cut their losses because they are right; people are stupid not to see things as they do, the market is wrong. And they spam financial market forums, always finding fault with the same things, in the hope that they can achieve their goals through a simple act of will.

If their script does not play out, they can even become verbally aggressive, those who don't share their opinion are ignorant. There is a form of "anorexia nervosa" among this type of trader, certainty replaces reflection and adaptation.

A blinkered trader has no chance of lasting on the financial markets because one of the most important characteristics of a financial market is that it is constantly changing and you must accept the idea of always putting your trading methods into question to try to change with it. Uncertainty and change control the financial markets. A blinkered trader filled with certainty will not survive for long in a changing world.

Since 2011 you have been able to see traders who continue to take bearish positions while financial markets increase in a straight line for over 8 months. 90% of these traders have disappeared, knocked out by a bullish market. These traders find it impossible to follow the first rule, they are not able to cut their losses, on the contrary, they tend to strengthen their position as if their conviction could influence the market in any way.

A trader with certainty is a condemned trader, trading teaches you one thing: the market is always right.

In compiling this brief overview of the pathological gambling trader, who looks for sensations before anything else, and the blinkered trader, who doesn't accept reality because he is blinded by his ego, I would like to ask you to think about what drives you, what drives us, to not follow our own trading rules, our Money Management, even though we know very well that it is this discipline that enables us to be winning traders in the long term. In my opinion, the hardest thing for a trader to do is accept that he is wrong and to be aware of the gambler that is in all of us.

So, to remind myself that my priority is not to lose money, I created this second trading rule to always remember the essential for me in my trading problem: I am here not to lose money and in the end, I make money.

35

RULE NUMBER 3 ONLY TRADE WHEN FIT

Trading is the most difficult and exhausting activity that I have ever practised. I have "been around the block"; I have been an IT engineer, an adult educator, a University professor, passing through less intellectual jobs such as farm labourer, market tradesman and I could go on. None of my previous experiences prepared me for the demands of the trading profession.

Trading is a mentally exhausting activity

After a day of trading from 10 am to noon, I am generally mentally exhausted. I practice scalping which is a type of trading that requires intense concentration and a rapid response capability. I can be concentrating for a long time with a finger on the trigger (the mouse), almost holding my breath, to find the best possible entry. I monitor 4 indices in real-time (Dow Jones, S&P 500, CAC 40 and Dax 30) in different time units. I must therefore permanently scrutinize about twenty charts and analyse common areas of support and resistance. This requires very special mental gymnastics and after a day of intensive trading, I am simply "empty", my brain is completely ready for a reality TV show.

Trading is a stressful activity

Beyond this mental fatigue, trading is an extremely stressful activity because we are constantly in the process of evaluating our decisions in real-time. Trading does not lie; it is either good or it isn't. This is its charm, we are fully responsible for our actions, each of our decisions has an immediate impact on our capital.

In case of a trading failure, when the situation is difficult to bear, some may collapse psychologically or find a scapegoat (the broker, Ben Bernanke, Mario Draghi, Goldman Sachs... the power of human imagination in these cases has always impressed me) to preserve an injured ego.

A large part of the stress comes from this psychological state, traders have too great a tendency to "be" their capital, to identify with it, to give it human "values" depending on their financial markets results. Trading is above all accepting the frustration and your own errors.

A trader is a top-level athlete

To try to limit stress and psychological exhaustion, and therefore play a lasting role, we should not hesitate to see ourselves as high-level sportsmen. Everything must be analysed, streamlined to be at the maximum of your physical and mental fitness to face the financial markets every day. A quiet working environment, optimized for its physical and visual comfort, limits fatigue and promotes concentration to a certain extent.

But you have to go further than that to last over time. At 45 years old, I no longer have the same energy as when I traded at 25 years old. I used to trade on the European and American markets from 9 am to 10 pm, sleep 4 hours and follow up with the Asian markets, go back to sleep for 2 hours and start a new cycle. That is a fantasy world now. I have learned to spare myself and above all listen to myself during the day.

So, at 4 pm, I make a sweet snack to bring energy to "my brain" because it is precisely the part of the day the densest in information and generally the most nervous with the first exchanges on the American markets. As an athlete, I avoid hypoglycaemia and I regularly feed my working tool, my brain (remember that even when at rest, the brain uses 60% of its glucose, so for a trader the rate must be very high).

Good physical and psychological states are essential for trading

Your form and psychological state are two crucial elements of trading. They are just as important as your capital and trading "method". In fact, when I am tired, I trade badly, it is indisputable, I tend to re-enter markets too quickly, I am more impatient, I risk getting too excited (my thrill blocker will be more easily overwhelmed), my analyses of the situation is poorer... and in the end, I lose money.

There is a direct relationship between my emotional state, my level of fatigue and my trading results. Also, I don't trade much on Fridays, nervous fatigue which accumulates during the week, makes me less able to trade effectively. When I didn't take this into account, Fridays statistically represented 40% of my loss-making days. By hardly trading on Fridays, my annual gains are higher than before, and I am less tired.

Therefore, each morning, I do my personal check-up, like a cyclist would check his bike. Fatigue? OK. Moral? OK. I can trade. If this is not the case, I don't trade, I rest, I take a break, I try to relax. It is a difficult discipline to have because we usually like trading, it is a type of addiction, we want "to be there". But the most sensible thing to do is to reinvest in your human capital, listen to it, let it rest to preserve its monetary capital. This should be the basis of each trader's Money Management.

When you decide to become a serious trader, it can radically transform your life. Personally, trading has enabled me to discover myself psychologically and it forced me, under duress, to have a better diet, a healthier lifestyle, to do a little sport, etc. even if it is still far from perfect. Trading has taught me to manage my human capital. My body and my mind are my working tools. They should be preserved because they are as important as my working capital. The two are intimately linked.

36

RULE NUMBER 4
DO NOT BE SWAYED

I have applied this rule for a few years, and coincidence or not, I have become a winning trader by applying it. I am not sure that this rule could apply to everyone. In my opinion, this depends on each individual's personality and psychology. In my case, it has enabled me not to be easily swayed and to abide by my swing trading objectives.

Previously, I spent a lot of time reading technical analyses, I spent many hours combing discussion forums and reading the specialised press... I felt that I was "working", collecting information, trying to see what the general trend was, etc. In fact, during the time I spent collecting information, I was trying not to think, to analyse my trades, contemplate my charts and specially to work on my behaviour and my psychology when I was positioned.

All the expended energy was, in fact, nothing more than perhaps a display of activity so that I didn't have to face the key point: trading success is 80% psychological. Worse, when I had a kind of conviction about the financial markets, reading 2 or 3 different opinions unsettled me and made me doubt.

Doubt is an essential part of trading, it enables you to stay cautious, to check your leverage, etc. but it can also have a negative effect, it can inhibit decision-making.

I got the bug a few years ago when I was preparing to place a buy on the Nasdaq 100 after several months of strong declines. I was confident of my analysis; it was essentially based on the recovery of a major psychological threshold with other supporting technical elements. A very nice swing to attempt.

Unfortunately, I read a few analyses with contrary views to my belief, I browsed a well-known trading forum where 95 per cent of the traders were bearish. I became doubtful, could I be right against everyone else?

I did nothing and I missed one of the best Nasdaq 100 recoveries in its history...which would have pretty much launched me as a trader on my own account.

From that day forward, I content myself with the raw information: the American unemployment figures, the GDP figures... I don't read, especially not interpretations, analyses... I have my personal opinion and above all, I look at how the financial market reacts when the information is released.

Too much information drowns information and adds fear

My behaviour is perhaps excessive, but I find there is a balance, a form of serenity. For example, I have been bullish on all indices since November 2011, it was my personal analysis that relied on market psychology and fear. I have a forum on my blog, Andlil.com, and read the comments. For months I had comments, sometimes harsh, of people who repeated what they had heard on the television.

I was obliged to justify myself because my opinion was opposed to the ubiquitous doomsayers forecasting the end of the world, the collapse of the Euro. They traded indiscriminately because X or Y analysts, recognised both figuratively and literally because they appear on television, repeatedly said that the indices were going to fall to their lowest historical levels.

We were simply in full mass hysteria or at least on the fast track to becoming an audience.

One fact must be considered: the business of television is to create fear among people because fear breeds an audience. There are many theses on this fascinating subject including in sociology and behavioural psychology. For example, if you say that the current crisis is not the mother of all crises but that it has been the economy's natural state for 40 years, that the Euro cannot collapse, etc.

This is of no interest, you will not appear on the TV, you will not be invited to a debate program. If you don't put on a show people will channel surf. If tomorrow you write a book entitled "Napoleon died a natural death" you are not going to sell a single book. If you publish a book called "Napoleon is dead, poisoned by the English", it will be a best-seller. The media give people what they want to hear, human nature is more attracted by fear, death, catastrophic situations, etc.

This must be taken into consideration in our trading, know how to judge the quality of information supplied to us and what motivates the media. In the end, the best interpretation is always our own. But to be able to really think, you certainly need to have a form of autism these days, otherwise, we can be totally overwhelmed by information of varying degrees of quality.

I also think that if I had not voluntarily cut myself off from these "influences", I would not have been able to hold my Bull position for as long as I did, and I would have missed the best 2 bullish years of this decade.

For a trader on his own account the essential objective is being free: no longer dependent on a boss, a hierarchy, being autonomous, responsible for his acts, his choices, etc. but intellectual freedom is also a guarantee of success in trading. In a nutshell: "Advice is cheap".

Always think for yourself.

37

RULE NUMBER 5 CONTROL YOUR LOSSES

One of the most important rules in trading is knowing how to control your losses and to keep pace with events. This is what generally makes the difference between a losing trader and a winning trader in the short, medium and especially long term.

Cut your trading losses or you are doomed

On my site's trading forum, almost every week you see people telling us that they have lost everything, that their account dropped to zero because they were unable to cut their losses, they waited for a turnaround in the market that could miraculously save their portfolio.

This attitude reflects a form of autism where we hold onto anything which could give us a little hope, we do not look reality in the face, we behave irrationally in the true sense of the word. We cannot afford to trade hoping for this type of event, it is unsustainable in the long term. We can be saved once, twice but one day or another, we won't be so lucky. It is absolutely essential to rid yourself of luck when trading, there is none, it doesn't have any effect, there are only positive and negative trades.

Why don't we cut our trading losses?

People give numerous reasons for their stubbornness in not wanting to cut their losses: cut your loss, it is often more painful narcissistically than for your wallet. In fact, here is where psychology plays a full part: trading is perhaps the only activity where we face the consequences of our choices in real-time. Trading is to constantly face a mirror which reflects what we really are, there is no escape.

In psychoanalysis, personal identity consists of 3 things: The Id (simply our unconscious), the Ego / Me (what we really are at one moment 'T'), the Superego (the limits that society imposes on us, our education, etc.). And to add spice to this delicate balance of contradictory forces which make up our personality, you need to add the ideal Me, which is what we would like to be.

Trading reflects us, sometimes brutally, what we really are. With each position we test the reality of the trader that we are, we test how our ideal Me compares to our Me. Because of this many traders will lose everything by not yielding, remaining inflexible faced with the markets because cutting their losses would be wrong and being wrong would damage their self-image, this would shatter their ideal Me, their Ego.

It is because of this that we sometimes find people who have been ruined on the financial markets and who are not going to stop telling you that they were right, that their analysis was good and that the market was either totally manipulated or that only idiots trade. It is simply a defensive reaction to protect their injured Ego, their ideal Me, blinded by reality. They do not want to look reality in the face, they avoid the mirror and so they need to find a scapegoat: the broker, the method used, the indicator, etc. which are inevitably bad.

An example of a controlled trading loss

Trade number 1 was made under the daily pivot point of the Dax 30 in anticipation of recovery on this support. The daily support, S1 served as a second area of possible recovery to exit flat. The value of this position was in the low spread between the daily pivot point and support 1 that could indicate a wide zone of elasticity to exit with a gain or flat.

Some bad news, Ukraine fell losing 60 points on the Dax, the expected recovery didn't happen, as soon as S1 broke, the loss was taken, that is - 22 points per lot. The scenario didn't happen as expected, we got out to take advantage of new opportunities.

If we had not taken this 22 point loss, it would have been - 82 points at the morning peak and -183 points at the end of the session, we would then have moved into "hope" mode in both situations.

By exiting, by accepting our losses, we were able to reposition ourselves on S2, we could operate on the market again and made a gain of 68 points per lot. Accepting a 22 point loss thus enabled us to get out of a delicate situation and reposition ourselves on a new opportunity chart. The balance is plus 46 points but above all the trader's working capital was not threatened by the "hope" mode that annihilates many traders every day. Taking losses is also a positive act in trading, it enables us to remain dynamic and not to miss a new opportunity because our capital is tied up in "hope" mode.

How to accept taking our trading losses

As we have seen, the psychological aspect is at the centre of being able to accept taking trading losses. There is no mystery, you have to work on yourself, on losses (symbolic and real) ... For this, psychoanalysis or psychotherapy can be of great help in identifying the reasons behind this narcissistic weakness.

Beyond trading, this also opens up opportunities for daring to do things. A lot of people are inhibited, fear of failure, of discovering that they will never be able to achieve their ideal Me, means that they do not act. French society does not value failure, it condemns it even though in the United States of America, for example, a person who has experienced many failures is valued, he is a veteran, he has dared to try, his status is raised.

It should, therefore, be acknowledged, that for a person it is often part of the accomplishment, to lose, to be wrong. I have rarely met people who are capable of saying: I was wrong, usually the prevailing opinion is: I was right, the others were wrong.

A person who can live of his trading is statistically exceptional they are among only 5% of traders. They have accepted the reality that they are not perfect, they never will be, they will still be deluded hundreds, maybe thousands of times...and that is of absolutely no importance. You must be totally uninhibited with regards to failure and when it arises, to accepting trading losses.

Doing this makes your management and abiding by your stops much easier.

Far too many people combine their social status, their profession and their trading results with who they are. A manager loses his job, a trader makes a big loss and these people fall to pieces, all their psychological structure collapses. Remember once again that we are more than our jobs, and that what we earn at the end of the month is not our identity. I am not a better person or intelligent because I made €10,000 on the financial markets in the month, nor am I pathetic and stupid because I lost that amount. You have to stop identifying with it.

You will know that you have made tremendous progress the day that a loss is no more than information like any other which doesn't change how you think about yourself. The same for a gain. A trader must strive toward psychological strength without weaknesses and for this, there is no mystery, you have to work on yourself. Trading can be the path to becoming a more balanced, more accomplished person, more than the path to becoming "rich".

I have, therefore, seen a psychoanalyst, this was my personal path, but there are equally people who understand, learn and try to master my impact, who accept that my ideal Me will always be inadequate and weak... and thus make losses, accept them, know how to recognise my mistakes without them being the end of my world.

My technique for cutting my trading losses

Technically, the bulk of my trading focuses on total control of my losses, any gains are “extra”.

This loss is a fixed monetary value. If during the day, I expect this level of loss, I close my position, I shut down my computer and I leave my home so that I am not tempted to continue. This gives me absolute and amazing comfort for my trading because I know in advance the maximum loss that I could make the following month if I lost for 22 successive sessions (which has never happened to me).

Few traders can say that in January my maximum loss will be: X% or X euros. And yet it is incredible psychological comfort, I no longer live with uncertainty, I know what I can lose every day, every week, every month. I know that this potential maximum loss will not put me in danger, that I will be there again the following month and the one after that, etc.

This technique of cutting my trading losses has other benefits:

I don't increase my daily loss by trying to "make up" for things. If I tried to make up for a significant loss, 9 times out of 10 I would only compound it at the end of the day.

I will not stupidly waste energy or stress and exhaust myself. I will be fresh in the morning, in full possession of my capabilities. Fatigue and stress management are essential factors for traders.

I leave a market that I don't understand in my time unit, I let it work without me thus giving myself the possibility of being in touch with it the next day.

This system works with iron-clad discipline, I no longer act like a child, not accepting losses or losing a game. Moreover, I am now no longer a "bad loser" of any game, it is the game that interests me, not winning or losing.

A bad loser has little chance of succeeding as a trader. I am satisfied when I make a good trade, regardless of the financial outcome, I am satisfied by "the act", the aesthetics of trading. There is beauty in trading.

In conclusion, if you can't manage to abide by your rules, your Money Management, if you don't look after your losses you will sink. You now know that you need to find a solution to discipline yourself, and especially to accept losses.

Loss is a normal, natural thing, we have come across it throughout our whole life, whether it is a financial loss, the loss of a loved one, loss of a job, the loss of social status or the loss of a favourite pen. You must learn to mourn and, for a trader, to narcissistically accept that you are not perfect and that a bad trade does not question who you are.

Acceptance of being wrong is what makes us adults, better traders and enables us not to be children any longer. Accepting to be wrong also allows us to no longer lock ourselves into our certainties, certainties that often prevent us from evolving. Trading is the pathway to becoming an adult.

38

RULE NUMBER 6 DO NOT FORCE YOURSELF TO TRADE

One of the most common errors that affect new traders, or even the most experienced traders, is to be on the market too much or even constantly. They run out of energy, they lose lucidity, and, in the end, they are much less efficient.

Trading is an addiction (like any other)

Let us not deceive ourselves, trading can quickly become an addiction in the same way as pathological gamblers in a casino, a bookmaker's, etc. Trading can easily become our drug of addiction, I still picture myself trading between 18 and 20 hours a day to do what I called a "World Tour": trading from 8 am until 10 pm on the European and American futures markets, then only sleep for a few hours and follow up on the

Kopsi in South Korea. I did this 5 days out of 7 then I would collapse and spend the weekend sleeping and thinking about the markets reopening on Monday.

What a drug! Trading can make us dependent because it gives us the very vivid and contrasting emotions of joy, fear, greed and at the heart of it all adrenaline. "Normal" life seems to us to be really dull, bland compared to what makes us live (and sometimes suffer), trading. You feel "alive" when you are positioned. Many traders haven't gone to these extremes as I have been able to do, trading more than 120 hours per week with sometimes more than 1,000 futures lots per day, but you find among almost all traders this need "to trade to feel alive". Our lives are sometimes so commonplace that trading is a safety valve, a "dream", the sensation of living a full life.

Trading is certainly more socially acceptable than taking drugs, but the cause of the addiction is the same in the end, a psychological problem, a narcissistic weakness, a want, artificially filled by trading. If you are in this situation, psychological work is essential to understand where this disorder comes from, and so manage to control it. To motivate you into taking this approach, I think that it is psychological work which was the most effective in enabling me to become a trader on my own account and to live comfortably from my trading. Through working on yourself more than on your indicators, your performance will be much better. Invest in yourself and the repercussions will be infinitely superior to your expectations, it will even affect your personality and your relationships with others.

Not being positioned is still taking a position

A lot of traders, who need their adrenaline rush, subconsciously force themselves to be on the markets. These are impulsive trades that you take out of boredom, through want, which are generally the most catastrophic and which will ruin your earnings for the day.

You need to accept this fact: not being in a position is still an act of trading. You are waiting for an opportunity, you regain strength, you think, you analyse market forces. Deciding not to enter a market because the trend isn't telling you anything is an act of effective trading, essential, key to the survival of your earnings. Often amateur traders force themselves to trade and this leads to disasters.

The difference between an amateur trader and a trader on his own account

There is a fundamental gap between a "punter" or amateur trader and trader on their own account. The first can "attempt big shots", have fun, they generally have a profession, a regular salary while the second risks physical survival every day. Let us make no mistake, trading is the only profession where one can find themselves on the street within 24 hours as a result of their positions being too strongly leveraged, poorly protected by guaranteed stops or hedged options. A football player can have a bad match, a baker ruins a batch of bread, etc. without ruining his life. A professional trader can lose everything overnight. There is insecurity and at the same time, there is an exhilarating side to being the master of your own destiny to such an extent.

I constantly sense this gap on my trading blog. I put my daily results there with account statements and an analysis of a few trades to provide educational content on real trading and not on theoretical trading. There is a large gap between the theory and the daily practice of trading. In short, a large part of the readers are amateur traders who trade a few hours per day at best. They are going to take a lot more positions to "offset" the fact that they are not able to be present as much as they would like, they will push the machine to the maximum and often it will explode in full flight.

I am often harassed by the same types of questions: Why don't you take more lots, why did you stop trading on Friday afternoon? Simply because a trader on his own account no longer attempts to make big "hits", or even to increase his capital at all costs, he looks for regularity before anything else, taking what he needs to live out of his capital each month. I consider my trading capital as my insurance fund, a life annuity. The act of switching from amateur trader to trading my own account has also changed my vision of trading significantly, I no longer only look for entries with low risk for scalping because I am perpetually on the markets, I can be there as much as my addiction requires of me.

Amateur traders carry on trading during the few hours that they can devote to trading as compensation, and also due to the frustration of having missed a particular market movement because they were visiting clients or attending an uninteresting meeting, etc.

Trade less to earn more

In the end, the quality of your trading is not only measured against the standard of living that it will allow you to assume, but also by the quality of life that it gives you. I advise amateur traders not to over trade, despite all the frustration that they may have by missing opportunities because of their professional lives. I was a teacher for 10 years; I am well aware of this frustration, meetings with students' parents while the Michigan index (which at the time was shaking the markets) was going to fall, a real ordeal.

Try to trade as if you were already trading your own account, only take good positions, if one evening you do not enter the market, it doesn't matter, there will be other evenings. By trading less, less impulsively, less with a sense of frustration, you will earn more and in the end, if your dream is to become a trader on your own account, it will get closer much more quickly, your working capital will surely and steadily increase.

39

RULE NUMBER 7
BREAK THE NORMAL RULES

It may seem strange to have a trading rule which says that we should not follow the rules. And yet, I think that there are "conventional" trading rules, commonly accepted, never questioned, applied by the vast majority of traders, which can be harmful to our results.

It is helpful to remember that over 90 per cent of traders lose money in the short and medium-term. If you take out beginner traders, who place bets (gamble) rather than trade, by badly managing their leverage and their emotions, there are still a large majority of experienced, seasoned traders who do not manage to produce regular gains over time. And yet, these are often encyclopedias of trading, they mastered all the theories, all the indicators, they have read hundreds of books on trading, etc. They dominate the subject perfectly and theoretically, they can give courses, but regular earnings are not there.

In fact, trading is much more than an accumulation of knowledge, which is, of course, essential for traders. However, in their case, too much knowledge kills knowledge. It leads to confusion for them because one indicator contradicts another, one indicates that they must begin to sell and take their earnings because the financial markets are overheating, another indicates that there is still room for an increase and chart analysis predicts a market collapse. You're on your own with all this.

For these reasons I strongly advocate that each trader establishes his own rules and abides by them (gains and regularity only come with the rigid application of these rules). The key to success in trading is custom made. All traders who earn their living with trading their own accounts all have this particularity: they think for themselves, they do not apply a "miracle" method, they have adapted their way of trading, to what they are, to their psychological ability, to their capital, etc. "Conventional" trading rules or methods are ready-to-wear, average methodologies that can apply to an average trader with average capital and typical psychology. We are worth better than ready-to-wear, ready-to-think, ready-to-trade.

You should take losses and let gains run

Some rules such as "you should take losses" have meaning and save your capital from ruin, but I suggest, as an example, questioning the continuation of this conventional trading rule: "let gains run".

I applied this rule for years and I lost money on the financial markets for years... because it doesn't apply to me at all. After more than 10 years of very regular losses, I decided to take a big-bang approach to my trading method and to throw it all out completely, everything that I had learned to do was of no use to me since I could not make regular gains.

Therefore I removed all the indicators that I had in front of my eyes, my trading charts looked like the dashboard of a Boeing, and after having analysed the tens of thousands of trades that I had made in recent years (a mammoth task which lasted 6 months), I discovered something which I had never seen with such clarity: 90% of my losing trades had been gains at some time.

For me, the "let gains run" turned into immense losses. On the strength of these findings, I devised a new rule tested my new rule: "you should take your losses and take your gains quickly"; and tested it for a few months. My new goal was, therefore, the following: as soon as my position had gained, I was ready to close even with a modest gain. The idea was that I should no longer turn a possible gain into an actual loss. "A bird in the hand is worth two in the bush."

You should take your losses and take your gains quickly.

By modifying this conventional trading rule, I have developed a very particular style of scalping that I call micro scalping. I scalp to earn on average between 1 and 2 points. Like this, I can trade 10 to 50 orders a day with a considerable degree of success. I now take my gains extremely quickly and this accumulation of micro-gains gives the right results at the end of the month with minimum risk.

In hindsight, when a position was gaining and it moved back to a loss, I psychologically had more difficultly to cash in my loss. I think this was because, subconsciously, I thought it was "unfair" and I focused on the idea that I was going to catch up.

And my loss increased. For 10 years lost money on positions which at some time had been positive.

I had to repeat this sentence hundreds of times to convince myself because it was the opposite of the conventional rule: "let gains run". A rule that I tried to follow in vain, and it cost me dearly. By closing these positions on even a small gain, I would have been able to save tens of thousands of euros, which turned into losses.

With this new trading rule, that I made to measure to compensate for my psychological weakness (namely: not being able to cash in a loss quickly when the position had been positive at a certain time). I do of course suffer from another type of frustration: I gain 5 points, as soon as it falls back to +1 point, I cash it in, and sometimes a few minutes later the position would have gained me +20 points.

But I manage to bear this frustration well because I know that this method enables me to earn money with extreme regularity and my psychology enables me to support this type of frustration easily. The cashed gained reassures me.

Of course, my intention is not for you to adopt the same rules of trading as me, that would have no meaning because you are not me: each person is unique, so you need to find your own rules. You came to trading as a unique individual.

Make sure you do not end up as a copy, because it will kill you. This means that you need to forge your own rules, your own tools. But perhaps you must also sweep aside the certainties that have been the mainstay of your trading for the year, to be more effective? At the end of the day, regardless of the manner, the verdict on the financial market, it has no appeal: with trading you make money, or you lose money.

40

THE TRADER'S RITUAL

Now that you have defined your money management, perhaps at the price of renunciation, and that you have engraved your trading rules in the Tablets of Law as intangible rules, I would like to talk to you about the daily ritual for a trader on their own account.

To be as efficient as possible, I have also established firm rules regarding my days' organization. My days are divided into periods and you will be able to perceive this as consistent with some of my trading rules.

This ritual of identical days is also done to reduce stress or anxiety. Everything is under control, known, controlled, repeated, the trader can, therefore, devote himself totally and fully to his charts.

There are therefore 3 levels that seem important to me for the trader: money management which secure the trading method, trading rules which make it possible to fight against the trader's biases and the rituals which secure the trader.

I'm going to describe my typical trading day, which may be off the beaten track. A specific thing about me is that I mainly do scalping which enables me to spend only a short time in front of my screens. A lot of people may think that I spend 12 to 14 hours a day in front of my screens because I trade European and American indices.

This is a totally mistaken view of scalping. Scalping makes it possible to concentrate on very short time slots while engaging in very high-intensity trading. Also, it is useful to remember that for 90% of the time, traders wait. Trading is above all about patience and avoiding trades taken out of boredom.

Like a sniper, scalpers and day traders wait for their target. In the end, they spend more time in a day doing something else (reading, writing, walking, thinking, cooking, etc.) than trading. Setting alerts is our greatest friend.

I, therefore, constantly focus on my psychological comfort to concentrate on the quality of my trading. So I try to trade only on time periods that I consider the most profitable (so as not to exhaust myself unnecessarily) and on levels identified in advance thanks to work on charts (so that I am not stressed, everything is planned). Nothing is improvised, everything is regulated and ritualized. It becomes automated like brushing your teeth.

I'm going to describe a typical day and then come back to some details that I think are very important:

From 7 am to 7:30 am: I wake up, take a cold shower to waken the body, I dress as if I were going to work (suit and tie) and I prepare a light breakfast.

From 7:30 to 8:00 am: I have breakfast, turn on the two trading stations (the main trading station and the backup trading station), look at what has happened during the night on the Asian markets by consulting the Reuters stock exchange briefing, and do my chart work, identifying levels that look interesting to me and noting them in my notebook. During this half-hour, most of the morning's work is done.

From 8 am to 8:40 am: I film 'Good Morning Trading' to share my morning preparatory work with people who follow me on the blog, the forum and the Andlil YouTube channel. Sometimes I make a trade or two but that is quite rare, the premarket is often very slow.

From 8:40 to 8:55 am, I dive back into the charts, reread the notes, visually memorize the levels I have identified, set my sound alerts and chat with friends on the forum.

From 8:55 to 9:00 am, I do five minutes of cardiac coherence exercises to relieve the tension, stress and excitement of beginning a day on the stock market.

From 9 to 9:30 am, very intensive scalping. If all goes well, I have finished my day (this means that I am satisfied with the monetary result, which enables me to move on to another phase of less intense trading).

From 9:30 to 10:00 am, less intensive scalping or, depending on the areas attained, attempt day trading and chatting with friends on the forum.

From 10 to 10:15 am, usually, if the market has stabilized, I take a break for a few minutes, prepare a green tea and walk around the living room to activate blood circulation, talk with my friends, etc. If something happens, my sound alerts warn me that I have to go back to the office.

From 10:15 to 11:30 am, I continue to trade, monitor, write, and chat on the forum while waiting for an opportunity. Eventually, if the day is done, I can go and do urgent daily tasks (pick up a parcel, do administrative necessities, etc.). My alarms are there so that I can trade out of the office if there are market movements.

From 11:30 am to 2:30 pm, this is what I call the 'soft underbelly'. It depends on the trading day.

If I feel that the market is quiet and that it is likely to stay that way, I adjust my alarms according to what happened in the morning and I can go for a walk, go swimming, write, read, chat on the forum, go to a restaurant, etc.

If I feel that the market has potential, that it is volatile, that it is likely to react because it is close to a key level, I stay alert and have lunch at home. Staying alert doesn't mean trading or blindly sitting in front of my screens with blinkered eyes. It means waiting for an opportunity to present itself while doing other things on my computer or at home.

At 2:30 pm., when there are important statistics in the United States of America, I am always in front of my screen looking for a nice opportunity. If there is one, I trade the European and/or American markets, if there are none, I go about my business until 3:25 pm, I write, I chat on the forum, etc.

At 3:25 pm, I do another five minutes of cardiac coherence exercises to relieve the tension, stress and excitement of the opening of the American market.

From 3:30 to 5 pm, I trade intensively in the European and American markets.

From 5 pm onwards, I start to slowly ease the intensity of my trading, cautious of the European, 5:30 pm closing. Generally, I will make myself a green tea and have a break, which means that I can take a walk and not take a position in the last half-hour. I start to review the European session, write down my impressions in my notebook, and debrief, breathing out the tension.

From 5:30 to 8 pm is the second slow period. I can trade American markets from 5:30 to 6:30 pm if there is still strength in the order book.

Otherwise, I sit in front of the TV, listen to a podcast, listen to music for background noise and write on my laptop while monitoring prices on my iPad. Sometimes I make an additional video for the YouTube channel to illustrate an article I have written.

If I haven't moved at lunchtime, I'll walk to do some shopping or do some aqua gym for an hour. From 7 to 8 pm, I cook and eat.

From 8 to 10 pm, I spend a quiet evening (Netflix, writing, discussion, etc.) while keeping an eye on the American stock market. Usually, I make a few trades during this time slot. But I always do two or three things at a time, I write, I listen to a show and I monitor the stock market. I always remain "active".

I, therefore, adapt my days according to current market conditions and volatility. People who do not trade may have difficulty understanding. I have no idea if I can go to a restaurant for lunch, if I can go shopping at 1:00 or 6:00 pm, it's the market that decides. I submit to its rhythm, to its breathing.

And all day long, I stay "connected" to the market from eight o'clock in the morning to ten o'clock at night. But that doesn't mean I stay in front of my screen doing only one task. I am constantly doing several things at once, trading is above all surveillance, and ultimately it is the least intensive, least time-consuming activity of my day.

Very exceptionally, I can trade non-stop from 3:30 to 10 pm, if the market allows it. It happens maybe five to ten times a year. But no matter what, I walk or do a sports activity for an hour a day. In the worst case, I force myself to go swimming, or rather, in this case, I splash around, from 10 to 11 pm to activate blood circulation. Effectively, if I trade from 3:30 to 10 pm non-stop, I am drained and have the energy of a snail.

From 10 pm to midnight is the decompression phase, I debrief from my notebook, I think about how to improve, usually, I read books or chat. I try to go to bed no later than midnight to get at least seven full hours of sleep after a hot shower to promote deep sleep and muscle relaxation.

This is my lifestyle from Monday to Friday. Sometimes, on Friday mornings, if I feel tired and that I need to breathe, I stop my trading week at lunchtime on Friday. I'll come back with more detail on the reasons why I avoid trading on Friday afternoons.

What to take away from this typical trading day

The first thing I think is important to note is that the real trading time, where it is the main activity, is relatively short. Between half an hour and an hour and a half in the morning when the European markets open, and between one hour and an hour and a half in the afternoon when the American markets open. In absolute terms, if I were not passionate about trading, if it were just a job I would like to ditch, my daily trading time would be limited to the time that the European and American markets open. I won't hide the fact that I would be deeply bored.

Every morning I do exactly the same thing: setting up, immersion, ramping up the tension to start trading. Then every night, I do the same thing again to bring myself down.

I try to have a balanced lifestyle: an intense trading phase in the morning followed by a rest phase to make myself "fresh" again for the afternoon when the American markets open. I try to get enough sleep to be on top form in the morning, I monitor my diet and hydration more and more.

I work on myself daily to try to improve myself by taking notes, meditating, trying to elevate my mind with adapted readings in the evening (because trading is at a very low neural level) and I constantly monitor myself. The cardiac coherence breathing techniques have enabled me to considerably improve my trading comfort, I'll come back to this later.

How to set up a typical trading day?

As you can see, nothing is left to chance. I traded for a decade when I was a teacher. I know that it is absolutely impossible to trade with such discipline in that situation. At the time, I was trading on the train with an unstable connection, I placed a few trades on the futures markets between 8 and 8:20 am before going to see my students, I tried to trade during my lunch break, etc. Obviously, a full-time trader on his own account can have better trading results, because his life is dedicated to the art of trading, rather than a full-time employee working in another field.

But trading is the art of constant adaptation. A trader never gives up, he adapts, he evolves, he looks for solutions. When I was a teacher, I tried to concentrate my teaching hours as much as possible in the mornings, I volunteered to work on Saturdays to free myself as much as possible for the American markets in the afternoons.

Having gone through these difficulties, I have very high regard for traders who do not have this as their main activity. Only enthusiasts can succeed and hold their own under these conditions. Unfortunately, I have no advice to give you because everyone has a very different professional activity.

Unlike a professional trader, you also have to control the risk of the environment. A professional trader creates his trading environment for himself while for you it is an additional imposed constraint. Colleagues who show up unannounced in the middle of a trade, a meeting that goes on later than planned, these types of events can prevent you from following the opening of the American markets when you had planned to exit your position.

In my opinion, you should concentrate on periods when you can stay calm, when you can analyse the market without being disturbed. But above all, don't force yourself to trade!

If you have a short time to trade, don't invent the opportunity to take a trade to avoid frustration.

Remember that not trading is still actively trading. It's a clear choice: I don't trade because if I buy or sell in this market, I'm not in an ideal situation. However, our objective is to take only quality trades, trades that we can explain, that have logic, consistency with the method. A trade that cannot be explained, whatever the result of that trade, is a bad trade. And trading is the quest for the perfect move, the quest for the perfect trade.

Not trading, not being in a position is an extremely positive act. There is something beautiful, poetic and almost sacred about respecting your methods and rituals.

Create a ritual when you trade. The repetition of the same gestures and situations allows you to enter your trading space little by little. You must be in your own bubble of the universe; you don't do anything anecdotal. You're going to trade. And that is very serious.

I think we often neglect those brief moments of concentration that allow us to get back into the situation.

It's up to you to create a ritual.

Green tea, for example, is very important in my ritual. It enables me to focus on the moment, feel the warmth of the chawan, be quiet and be ready to start my cardiac coherence exercise that will totally relax me before the financial markets open in the morning in Europe and the afternoon in the United States of America.

THE PSYCHOLOGY OF TRADING

Suffer

41

THE CRUELTY OF REALITY

You have searched long and hard for a proven trading method while using your demo account.

You then took the trouble to regulate it by precise money management and you frame yourself each day using your rituals and trading rules. And yet the results are not at all what you had hoped. This is what I call the cruelty of reality. You have searched, persevered and now you are in the suffering phase.

If it's any consolation, all traders have gone through this phase: doubt, devaluation, the desire to give up and abandon trading altogether.

You don't understand why you can't apply your simple rules.

Why you don't stand by your maximum daily loss.

Why you took that meaningless trade out of boredom that ruined your day.

Why, but why did you trade during a central bank announcement when all the professional traders told you that you should avoid it like the plague?

Why did you take that little extra trade on a Friday night to round out your winnings that wiped out your week?

But why do any of these things?

I think you'll recognise yourself in some of these questions, there's no need to add to them. I can tell you only one thing: Hang in there!

It's time to search and persevere again. Because you have progressed considerably, take the time to see how far you have come even if the results frustrate you.

I have met hundreds of traders who had outstanding demo results, and all of them, without exception, have "consumed" the real thing in their heads. Because trading is not just your trading method and money management. It is, above all, control of your emotions, your impulses, it is to remain invariably in control of yourself.

Clearly, I consider my trading method to be only 10% of the work. The implementation of money management, rituals and trading rules accounts for 30%. And 60% of your job is to control your emotions, work and strengthen your psychology.

You can be lazy, scared, etc. you can go through a complete cycle again, change your trading method, change your money management, change your trading rules, etc. This will change absolutely nothing because you will come back to "real life", to face who you are, to face your emotions, to simply face your personality. In trading, there are no lies. You make the decisions, there's no convenient way to offload on a colleague, the company, the government, etc.

Of course, some people try to find a scapegoat for their actions: it is the broker's fault, a conspiracy of multinational banks to trigger their stop loss and steal €500.

This is a defensive process, the person suffers, his ego and dreams have been shaken and the only possibility left psychically is to discharge his responsibility. It is expelled like this. It's also very much in the spirit of the times, we live in an increasingly childish society where we expect far too much from the state, which has to find work for us, feed us, etc. and if people don't succeed, it's always someone else's fault.

To me, this is typical teenage behaviour, always trying to run away from their responsibilities. But being a grown-up isn't running away. Don't run away from what just happened, your stock market crash. This is a necessary and mandatory step to moving forward. You finally get into the "hard" part of the subject, in the 60%.

There are different schools to explain what we all go through in trading.

Some schools such as neurobiology explain that the fight is hard because it is unequal. The neocortex (which enables us to analyse) must master two other brains: the limbic (which manages emotions and we are often overwhelmed by emotions when we trade) and the reptilian (which manages instincts, the most primitive). It's imperative that the neocortex can dominate.

For my part, intellectually, I am closer to the Freudian movement. But I want to make it clear that all these schools of thought are right. Again, we are all unique and no one knows the entire truth.

I think trading is one of the few activities that makes us face ourselves. We can't run, we can't hide, we can't backtrack, we can't let go of the guilt and that's what makes trading so painful and so exciting.

We have a choice:

Either we remain in a logic of repetition, repeating the same mistakes, by ignoring the trading method and/or money management, or we accept the idea that the problem, that the weak link is us (this is what made me waste 10 years, believing that it was the method that was bad, not me).

And then trading suddenly takes on another dimension. It's a great tool for personal development. Trading enables me to discover myself, to discover my impulses, my anxieties, my fears and to question myself deeply. It's a big upheaval because you don't come into trading at all for personal development. You come here to make money.

But to make money sustainably and regularly, you have to learn how to control yourself, you have to know how to manage your emotions, you have to not get excited when you win and be on the verge of depression when you lose.

At this point, you can either choose to go back to the method of thinking that the trading method is wrong and turn a blind eye to the psychology part of trading, or you can decide that if you have "faltered", that if you are not able to follow your own rules (and I insist, no one has imposed them on you), then there is indeed a problem that needs to be addressed.

In the following chapters, I will offer you a few ideas to try to improve your trading skills.

You have to ask yourself how much stress you put on yourself with leverage. Doesn't it cause too much anguish and frustration?
Trying to figure out why you're cracking up?

How can you quickly digest these unpleasant psycholo-gical situations to move on and advance?

And finally, a few leads that I was able to find to progress psychologically. But as for the trading method, and since we are all different, these are more avenues for reflection. But in any case, you have just discovered the submerged surface of the iceberg in trading.

Being almost a caricature, a trader with a strong psychological balance will be able to make money with any trading method as long as he is disciplined and can apply his money management and trading rules. A trader with the best trading method in the world (if it exists) will never be able to make money if he is not able to follow his money management and trading rules.

It's probably hard for some people to hear, but I think that deep down you know that the problem is not the method but the man.

Once again, I wish you great courage and perseverance!

42

STRESS IN TRADING

Why should you try to reduce stress in trading to improve your results and reduce psychological pressure?

Trading and the levers (of stress)

I am often asked why I don't take (more) leverage based on my results?

The answer is simple, to reduce stress.

I "struggled" in the financial markets for years because I did not have enough capital, I used leverage, I did warrants, options, Clickoptions in their era, etc. In short, I had to take risks to build up an acceptable capital balance and I took monumental hits, sometimes destroying several months/years of work.

I have had scary positions, sleepless nights, dreadful weekends and hours where you end up screaming and crying about having wiped out your working capital, your savings.

But once there is enough capital, leverage (and stress) can be reduced or even eliminated. Of course, you don't optimize your capital but you take less risk, you are no longer in a strategy of capital accumulation, but of cash extraction (taking inflation into account) and in the end, trading becomes a real pleasure and not a need.

This is the paradox: it's at the beginning, when you have little capital, the less experience you have, the more risk you have to take. When you have enough capital, the overall results improve, if you decrease leverage, because in my case, I trade "serenely" (with reduced but still present stress, losses still hurt) without leverage but if I traded as before with leverage of 3 5 10m etc. the stress would increase exponentially.

That's why trading is very enjoyable now, whereas for a very long time it was painful.

This stress is, in fact, a signal from our body, we are simply afraid (and rightly so), so the awareness of danger makes us develop "abnormally".

Neurobiology contributions to Trading

There are exciting neurobiology studies on this theme, they show that in situations of extreme stress (taking leverage of 10 is an extreme situation for your capital, a small flash crash like in 2010 and you have nothing left) decision-making abilities are disrupted, the brain unconsciously tends to do everything it can to stop this stress.

As I read this, I had an epiphany. When I was leveraged, I often unwound a negative position despite common sense (traditionally, at the highest or lowest point of the session, sometimes knowing it very well). In fact, our body and brain are trying to lower stress. Closing a position puts an end to this unbearable stress and you then feel a form of relief (end of stress) even if you may become angry or cry (decompression phase) faced with the pitiful result.

Psychoanalysis' view of stress and Trading

In Freudian psychoanalysis, stress is managed by the protection shield, a sort of psychic wall, a dam that makes it possible to contain and control libidinal energy.

It is this that prevents you from physically attacking your neighbour or your boss, if the dam overflows you can control yourself from taking action or in the case that concerns us "slipping" on the financial markets: moving from 2 to 20 leverage to "rebuild" despite everything, common sense, your money management, in short, a capitalist suicide.

You have to keep an eye on your protection shield every day to optimize your trading and avoid the bad day when a slip wipes out your capital. The protection sheild fluctuates over time (you are tired, it is reduced, you are more impulsive, more aggressive, etc.). That's why, ideally, if you don't feel well, you shouldn't trade despite the temptation (trading addiction).

Moreover, we must avoid triggers, which generate greater stress because our analytical capacities are impaired. If there is a stress peak our brain does everything to reduce this stress and this can result in a disastrous exit from the market.

In my opinion, psychology is central to successful trading, "techniques and methods" are only lures because personal experience, feeling the markets and your own emotional management are much more important.

When I took my trading journal and put it in parallel with my personal diary, I saw a lot of connections: the days of big losses corresponded to "arguing with my girlfriend, waiting for scary blood results, etc.". The parallel between personal states and trading results is systematic. I didn't find any bright days in the financial markets when I was down.

So, if I had handled my protection shield better, I would have avoided these losses by not trading. Besides, there are very few days when I've made a lot of money by "being bad".

You, therefore, need to bring together protection shield management and money management and to do everything so that you have as little pressure as possible.

In my case, I reduced unpleasant stress by reducing leverage. By being better in my head and, therefore, in my trading my results have certainly been better than if I had continued to trade with high leverage.

So, we have to look for our acceptable stress level, our personal parameter. With the same capital, some traders will use a leverage of 5 with confidence and others will be on the verge of psychological collapse with a leverage of 2.

Again, I draw your attention to your uniqueness

Just because trader X trades leveraged at Y with a capital of W doesn't mean you can do the same. You are not X, it's up to you to discover your rules in the face of stress. It must be high enough for you to be stimulated and low enough for you to trade serenely to retain all your abilities. You don't trade on an empty stomach nor one filled with fear.

Please note:
This stress may also explain the fact that often large bank traders who set up their own fund don't succeed. The stress is much greater when it comes to your own money than it is with other people's money. Working in a bank, at worst you risk being laid off and unemployed, but as a proprietary trader at worst you end up on the street.

To paint you a picture, when we trade with high leverage, it's a bit like wanting to drive a car full pelt around a racetrack.

We realize that we can't drive at 300 km an hour for hours without risking an accident. We modulate our speed and sometimes peak at 300 km an hour on the straight while modulating our speed on the rest of the track.

We should do the same thing in our trading.

Trading with adapted leverage that gives us low stress and from time to time, exceptionally, on rare configurations with very high performance, allow us, if we feel able, a small speed spike. But driving at 300 km an hour all the time, trading with high leverage all the time, the result is the same: you crash head first into the wall.

A good idea to reduce stress in trading: if you trade at €25 per point on the Dax 30 and you don't feel comfortable, switch to €5 per point with Dax mini lots.

You enter in the same way and if your trade succeeds, you can reinforce it by taking a second Dax 30 mini lot. You are then at €10 per point without too much stress. You may even be able to get better results than if you continue to trade at €25 a point while being stressed.

Now that we've understood that we can't drive at full throttle all the time, that the stress is too high, we realize that this inevitably creates frustration within us.

Reality does not bend to our desires. After so much work and research to develop my trading method, my money management, my rituals and rules, here I am blocked by my own psychological limits. What frustration!

Now let's ask ourselves about frustration in trading which is our daily lot.

43

FRUSTRATION IN TRADING

Frustration in trading is responsible for a lot of losses. Numerous traders lose their means because of frustration. They take a trade out of boredom, they enter the market outside of their trading method because they want, for example, to quickly recover a loss that they have trouble digesting, etc. Trading is to be permanently frustrated. You have to accept it and live with it. There is no choice.

"Good" psychological balance enables good self-control, it also enables you to adhere to your trading and money management rules. The trading method is thus respected.

By being barely caricatured a trader who is not psychologically in control loses no matter what method he uses and no matter what trading rules he does not follow. Eventually, he cracks, freaks out, etc. One of our worst enemies in trading is frustration.

What is frustration?

Frustration is a negative feeling that human beings develop according to circumstances. It is above all a dissatisfaction. It refers to any impossibility for a person to appropriate what he desires, what he covets.

These frustrations and dissatisfactions occur daily in all human beings and in all areas.

No matter what the professional field, you can have the dissatisfaction of occupying a position that is uninteresting, sentimental (I won't go into more details), social (being frustrated with your social "position"), the frustration of not earning enough money and not being able to buy the latest fashionable gadget when John was able to buy it for himself (which is deeply unfair), etc.

Human beings are therefore constantly in contact with this frustration, it is a very basic, very childish feeling. From the very first minutes of our lives, we are dissatisfied, the baby cries and screams because he is hungry.

In short, we are constantly bathed in this dissatisfaction which causes a lot of frustration because the world is not as we would like it to be. So we find the world unjust and that creates other negative feelings, jealousy, bitterness, etc. and yes, when we were the darling of our parents, the centre of the universe, having reached adolescence, we had to make this terrible observation: we are not the centre of all things, the universe does not revolve around us. And there goes the ego, all put in its place.

What is frustration in trading?

Frustration in trading is certainly one of the most harmful elements for our financial markets' results. It's important to understand that no one will ever be a perfect trader.

I must have done over 100,000 trades in my life; I remember doing a perfect trade just once. I once bought at the lowest price of the day and sold it almost at the highest of the day. A moment of perfection, I got my blue note, the trader's perfect moment of grace. I'm certainly never going to see that again.

It must be understood that every trade and non-trade carries its own intrinsic dose of frustration. The trader has to live with this frustration all the time, it is consubstantial to trading.

You have to stop telling yourself the following:
"Oh, if I'd kept it longer, I'd have made a lot more money! "or "oh if I hadn't hesitated and had entered!" and replace them with "Great, I made a gain, I'm happy" or "great, I hesitated, I listened to myself, that's good, I've progressed".

You made choices; those choices seemed right at the time. You took them knowingly, nobody put a gun to your head.

If you don't accept it, you remain at the stage of adolescence or childhood where the adolescent thinks he is all-powerful.

To become an adult is to accept one's fragility, one's shortcomings, one's mistakes, etc. and that the adult is not the centre of the universe. Besides, the universe and the financial markets don't even know he exists.

Therefore, you have to accept frustration as a natural part of trading. It is always there, perpetually there to belittle our ego if it's too strong.

Traders have to accept frustration

To become a better trader, you have to "grow up". Accept this frustration as a natural part of our trading.

And besides, if we go a little bit further, accepting frustration is a very important part of educating children so that they won't be unhappy when they grow up.

Children who have never been frustrated, child kings will never make good traders, or at least they will need to reprogram themselves completely.

How do you fight against frustration in trading? The protection shield is our dam to keep us from cracking under the blows of frustration.

44

THE PROTECTION SHIELD AND TRADING

The protection shield is a term used by Freud in some of his works, notably in Beyond the Pleasure Principle and Inhibition, Symptoms and Anxiety.

The "protection shield" is to protect the organism against excitations from the outside world which, by their intensity, could destroy it. This definition is the one given by Catherine Audibert in L'incapacité d'être seul, Payot & Rivages, 2011, which I find very eloquent.

Indeed, we are constantly being solicited, stimulated and attacked by the outside world. It can be loud and constant noise, hurtful words, etc. And we "take it" all the time without giving in to our frustrations and disappointments, which makes us civilized beings.

The protection shield can be thought of as a dam that protects us from the outside world. Aggressions, impulses, frustrations and tensions crash down on this dam. It lessens the impact on us. But if the dam cracks, we are then "overwhelmed" by our emotions and we break: anger, shouting, violence are then our only means of expression. Generally, we break when faced with situations that we have already experienced hundreds of times without flinching. But on that one day, at that one point, our protection shield is no longer enough to take it. The dam breaks and there is an outburst.

A trader's external stimulations

When we are in front of our screens, we are bombarded with information from our charts. We try to understand the market, to see the trend. We're in a state of intense and permanent brain activity. But, when we're in a position that is when our protection shield is needed most.

As our position changes, we feel and receive a lot of stress, emotion, excitement and frustration. The risk is that our protection shield will be overwhelmed by this flow and we will lose our footing. This is what traders sometimes call the tilt. They just crack under the pressure; their dam is broken.

We have all experienced being overwhelmed by events in a losing position from which we could not exit. We let it get worse and worse until, usually, we take our loss at the lowest point of the day, when our protection shield gives way.

But, contrary to popular belief, we can also lose our footing on a winning position. There is also the possibility of receiving too much stimulation with a winning position, which can overwhelm our protection shield. We then cash in the earnings too quickly. But also, too excited and overwhelmed by the amounts gained, we may increase the lot size too much on the next trade. This is also a sign that our protection shield is overwhelmed.

The trader's duality

Indeed, what I think is important is to realize that when we trade, we have to be two people at the same time. A trader who analyses his charts and also a coach, a trainer who analyses the emotional state, the strength of the trader's protection shield.

A trader is like a football player who wants to play in a match. But the coach tells him to get off the field because he's not fit to play football anymore. We have to be our own coach to keep an eye on ourselves all the time. Before entering each trade, we must ask ourselves these questions: am I fit to trade? What condition is my protection shield in?

Within this perspective of mastering and controlling the situation, it is worthwhile to constantly monitor yourself and check the strength of your dam, your protection shield, so as not to collapse during the next trade.

How to strengthen your protection shield?

If it is worthwhile to detect your possibility of cracking while trading in advance, which enables you to get out of the field before a disaster strikes, it is just as worthwhile to reinforce your dams.

There is no miracle method, personal psyche has a lot to do with it, this is your dam's foundations. Some people can naturally handle a lot of stress, external aggression and frustration without any particular reaction. Others instantly become angry and react to the slightest frustration. Strengthening foundations requires a great deal of personal work and learning to "cash in" and accept frustration.

But even with weak foundations, you can strengthen your dams. It is vital to sleep well; sleep is one of the keys to not cracking. A healthy and balanced life naturally strengthens the protection shield.

But what secures the dam is, above all, prevention. If you don't feel well, if you've just argued with your partner, you mustn't even think about trading. We only start trading when our protection shield is stable when it hasn't already been used. You don't trade angry, you don't trade tired, etc. because that's likely to end up breaching the dam and be a catastrophe for the wallet.

Conclusion on the Freudian protection shield

Freud in his psychoanalytical theory said very little about the protection shield. It is not a major element in his thinking, but it can be appreciated for its simplicity and effectiveness.

We have within us a dam that supports us, that can withstand outside events. We have to take care of it so that we don't sink and be swallowed up by our emotions and frustrations.

A strong protection shield keeps the situation, our trading, under control. But it's a shifting dam that is more resistant or less resistant depending on our health, our relationships, etc.

Therefore, like a coach watching his football player, you have to watch it constantly to assess its strength.

For a framework to be remembered, we should only trade when we are neutral or centrist.

If we are too far to the left (if we are down in the dumps, if we are depressed, if we have personal problems for example) or too far to the right (if we start to feel strong and invulnerable in our trading, a situation that can happen to a scalper who chains a hundred trades without loss), it is better not to trade and take a break until we become centrist again.

Neither too left nor too right, the middle way, the balance of power. Whatever the market situation, we must always and permanently dominate, control and accept this inevitable share of frustration. You have to kill "the ideal trader", our imaginary ideal of ourselves and return to the reality that we can improve.

I can become a rigorous trader, managing my stress and accepting my frustration but I will never be a perfect trader. It makes me dream less, it makes me frustrated, my childhood dream is slipping away, I won't be a Super Trader with superpowers but I'm not here to dream anymore. I'm here to make money, to do the job like a pro, as efficiently as possible with my weapons: my broker, my trading station and myself.

And if we have a major loss, we need to grieve as quickly and effectively as possible and keep moving forward.

A friend once told me, “Suck it up and move on.” Kill Eeyore and get on with it.

Now we are going to look at the grieving process.

45

GRIEF IN TRADING

The 5 phases of grief that Kübler-Ross applied to trading

Elisabeth Kübler-Ross was born on 8 July 1926 in Zurich, Switzerland, and died on 24 August 2004 in the United States. She was a psychiatrist specializing in palliative care for people at the end of life.

Her theory, known as the Kübler-Ross model, analyses the different stages people go through when they learn of their impending death. This theory has spread to all forms of catastrophic loss because the symptoms are very similar from one person to another and from one violent trauma to another.

The Kübler-Ross model, therefore, has a "universal" application appeal.

Kübler-Ross' 5 phases of grief are:

1. Shock, surprise, denial
2. Anger
3. Negotiation
4. Depression
5. Acceptance

The application of Kübler-Ross' phases of grief in trading is fundamental. It is important to be able to determine quickly what phase you are in following a capital loss to avoid the worst.

Shock, surprise, denial in trading

This is a relatively short phase of astonishment. Usually, that's when you cash in your loss. The extreme stress of managing a difficult stock market position disappears, you go out, you take your loss, there is no more position.

You are in a state of shock, drained, flabbergasted as if paralyzed, frozen in front of your screen. You're still in denial. No, it can't be! The mind refuses the reality of loss. This phase is quite short.

Anger in trading

This phase comes quickly and abruptly. It's the reaction to the shock. The reality of loss is obvious. A feeling of injustice appears, "but why me?", "This is not fair" and aggression is unleashed irrationally. Shouting, screaming, but above all searching for a scapegoat and the desire for revenge in the face of this perceived unjust situation are common.

Traders then invent conspiracies aimed at them personally, looking for those responsible to clear themselves of guilt (the broker, politicians, the stock analyst who said in the morning that...). Blinded by anger, unable to take stock, they are overwhelmed by their emotions and their behaviour is generally irrational.

This is the most chaotic period with irrational phases of anger towards other people. The person gives the impression of being unstable and is desperately trying to shake off the guilt.

Self-negotiation in trading

After understanding the inability of anger to solve the problem, negotiation emerges. The desperate person asks destiny or divine bodies to intervene, we try to find a solution to escape the news we don't like. You can even try blackmail like a young child, trying to find "miracle solutions".

A trader will sometimes look for a miracle method in trading to "rebuild" himself. Before we were in the instinctive or emotional reactions, the negotiation phase marks the beginning of being aware of reality.

The depression phase in trading

When reality imposes itself, when the illusion of miracle solutions has run its course, when the trader stops lying to himself, depression shows up. It's the longest phase.
The person falls into heavy despair due to a feeling of powerlessness and strong guilt. The devaluation phase emerges, "I suck", "I'll never make it". It constantly replays the causes of the trauma, it relives it again and again, it goes on and on in a loop in the past. There is no more looking for an external scapegoat, it is the beginning of accepting your actions and responsibilities.

Acceptance of loss in trading

This is the final stage of grief, the rebuilding phase. Once the feeling of helplessness caused by the loss is accepted, the trader begins to understand and accept the reality of the loss. He then begins his reconstruction. The trader is then able to assimilate what has happened and to project himself towards the future by reinterpreting in a more positive way what has just happened without childishly blaming others. The person can then rebuild and move forward as an adult.

In the case of a trader, he reviews his money management, understands why he slipped, etc. and transforms this loss into an opportunity to progress and not to lament his fate.

The limits of Kübler-Ross' theory

It is important to note that these phases may vary from one individual to another with possible backtracking to a previous phase. Behaviour is different depending on these phases of grief, some people need to isolate themselves and others need to surround themselves. Each human is unique, he reacts differently to the same traumatic event, but he goes through these different phases faster or more slowly.

Conclusion on Kübler-Ross' 5 phases of grief applied to trading

It is important for a trader to be aware of Kübler-Ross' 5 phases of grief and to apply them to his trading. This will enable him to overcome the micro-defects of his losing positions more quickly and so remain an efficient trader.

In the event of a large loss, you must, of course, stop trading. Phases 2, 3 and 4, anger in trading, the negotiation phase and depression are the most dangerous times for a trader on his own account. That's where he can blow his money management to smithereens and hit the floor. When you feel that you are losing your footing, that you are overwhelmed by events, that your protection shield is collapsing, you must shut down your computer and leave the room.

If you only remember one thing from this chapter, it's this one. This is the absolute red alert; you can do anything at this point and wipe out years of work. Whatever you have lost if you stay, you will multiply it.

As soon as your protection shield is overwhelmed and you are in phase 2, 3 or 4 of the Kübler-Ross phases of grief, you can slip at any second. There's only one thing to do, leave, run away from your trading desk. Your future survival as a proprietary trader is at stake.

Rest assured, we are going to look at how we can strengthen ourselves to progress and become mentally stronger.

46

STRENGTHENING AND PSYCHOLOGICAL TRIGGERS

In this chapter, I am going to tell you what I experienced in my trading career, how I was able to strengthen myself psychologically and what were my main triggers. I hope that this might say something to you, give you some leads.

There are a lot of ways to strengthen your protection shield to manage stress in trading better.

It is worth remembering that a healthy lifestyle can make a difference. The activity of a trader is not particularly physical, sitting in his chair and waiting, I have known more physically demanding roles. But it's a particularly nerve-wracking activity. And nothing beats a good night's sleep. There are so many times in my trading diary that I see a connection between too little sleep and a difficult day in trading. Tired before you start trading, the day is already laid out before you.

To relieve stress, everyone has their own method, from meditation to sports to yelling at their children. It's up to each person to manage stress according to his personality.

For me, being a trader and scalper, I look for quick, practical solutions. I will share with you a solution that I recently discovered that allows me to release stress and concentrate before each intensive trading phase.

Cardiac coherence

For a long time, I looked for ways to reduce my tension and stress when I trade. One of the biggest advances I've been able to make was to accept that I could make less by reducing leverage. And maybe not so surprisingly, I started making more. Probably because I was more relaxed and not subject to the market anymore.

I felt that I was missing something to perform really well. I tried meditation, sports, special food, but they didn't suit me, they were too long, too complicated, too time-consuming. I discovered cardiac coherence exercises a few months ago. I tested them without really believing in them and I must admit that I can't do without them anymore.

They are breathing exercise of childlike simplicity. This helps to regulate stress and anxiety in an extremely effective way (at least in my case).

Three times a day, just take six breaths a minute for five minutes. And that's it. I let you read about the technique on the net, there are complete websites dedicated to it and which explain in detail the benefits of doing these exercises.

Concretely for trading, I do them just before the opening of the European markets in the morning and the opening of the American markets in the afternoon. I downloaded a free application on my iPhone that tells me when to breathe in and when to breathe out. And, in this way, at 9:00 and 3:30 I am in a state of calm and concentration rarely equalled. I used to be very impatient before the markets opened but now, I come to them in a state of calm.

And now, when I feel a peak of stress, I focus on my breathing again for a minute and it disappears. You should try it.

Watching yourself

Another technique that has helped me progress is to watch myself trading. I installed a webcam and filmed my charts and reactions. Then I saw my tension, my stress, my anxiety, my anger, etc.

It was a kind of trigger; I saw myself in so much pain that I thought I absolutely had to react. I didn't even realize it. This was in a way the "shock of reality". I've made a list of software in your private area that lets you film yourself.

In the same vein, I have a friend who didn't know if he was really stressed. He had a form of resistance; he couldn't perceive if he was in a good state to trade or not.

The trick was to use a connected watch used by the joggers. When his heart rate is too high, the watch starts beeping. If the watch emits a sound, he is prohibited from trading, he waits for his heartbeat to drop. Simple and effective. It doesn't help him to be less stressed, it is an automatic form of monitoring his state as a trader.

Question yourself before you enter a trade

I would like to emphasize this simple idea, which can be incredibly effective. A trader wears two hats: he is a trader and at the same time his own supervisor, his own career head-warrant officer, his own coach, etc. you name it. He has to watch himself, control himself, he's never safe from a slip.

To do this, I always ask myself two questions before taking a trade, a sort of filter:

Am I fit to trade?

Is the trade worth it?
It takes a second, but I've reduced my lousy trades considerably because of it.

I was able to eliminate the trades taken out of boredom, out of spite, out of revenge by saying to myself "no, I'm not in a state to trade" or "no it's not worth it, if I do it I would be a fool". This jerks me back to reality and so enables me not to trade and to solve this psychic conflict.

Another example: a few years ago, I was sometimes a compulsive trader. I found a trick to "get around" this compulsion. I opened a mini account representing less than 1% of my capital and when I felt overwhelmed, a desire to be on the market at all costs, I would place an order on my micro-account and so my tension was released. That compulsion finally passed. All this shows that we can try to find techniques to "tame" our weaknesses.

Need help?

Sometimes it saves time to get help. This is a hypothesis that should not be overlooked. Once again, there is something for everyone, for every purse and for every trend.

If you manage to get further along this road, trading in your life will be more than just a way to try and make money, it will be a real personal development tool. You will want to discipline yourself, to control yourself, to understand why when you trade you feel so many emotions, impulses, etc. For that, you have all the shrinks possible (psychiatrist, psychologist, psychotherapist, psychoanalyst, etc.). I will not venture in this book to praise one profession over another, it is still a sensitive issue.

Do not be alone

I think it is extremely important not to be isolated in trading but to share as much as possible of your joys, sorrows, questions, anxieties, successes, defeats, changes; etc. That's why I created the Andlil.com forum because I felt particularly isolated as a trader on my own account.

At the time I spent my days in front of my computer and, to avoid boredom, trading, I played network games 12 hours a day while monitoring the stock market. After a few months, I decided to do more positive things than killing the same virtual wolf 7,857 times.

The forum lets you discuss your day with other traders who feel and understand what you are saying. Because in everyday life it's extremely complicated to explain to your friends that you've had a wonderful week because you've had a bounce on the S2 M of the Dax 30 that you've been waiting for for 10 days, which allowed you to have a safe TP + 40 and the possibility to aggressively chain pyramid trading to try to reintegrate the S1 M. You'll be taken at best for quirky at worst you'll create a void around you.

It is just as important to choose your environment wisely. This is often the mistake of beginners who, out of fear and perhaps gregarious instinct, keep to themselves. This simply reinforces their weaknesses. Never in history have we seen people who are bad at maths get together and manage to understand maths. You need to seek out people who can raise you, who can allow you to progress.

Your trading patterns can have a major impact on your trading results. Absolutely flee from moralists and people who are jealous of you because you are a trader. The only effect this has on you is to pull you down. Remember one thing, a lot of people can't stand traders or other successful people. Spare yourself these social tensions that can only bring you disruption in your trading.

In my book, "Traders are True Communists", I talk about the problem of relationships with others, about the constant obligation to explain that if the world is not going well, if there is unemployment, if people do not have the life they dream of, those responsible are not the scapegoat traders. I wrote this book to give proprietary traders arguments to explain what they do, how they live and how they are more useful to society than 90% of the people who criticize them. I was tired of hearing the same stupid things about traders, the financial markets, etc.

Robin Hood was a Trader on Amazon

Some psychological triggers

I think that for a lot of people they move forward suddenly because of a trigger. At least in my life, I've often functioned like that. There are breaking moments that change everything.

In my life as a trader, there have been three important triggers that have made me significantly progress psychologically in my life and my trading.

Trigger number one

You have to follow the trend and stop being frustrated. I had this huge annoying defect of knowing that when the stock market went up, I sold and when it went down, I bought. Looking back, I realized that I was still a mental "teenager" when I was doing this. I needed to oppose to prove things for sure. I did a huge amount of personal work, which allowed me to understand why I was in "opposition", why I had this annoying bias in the stock market.

Now I have no bias. The stock market goes up for 10 years. I buy for 10 years. The stock market goes down for 10 years. I sell for 10 years. I no longer choose my side between buyers or sellers; I have abandoned this logic of support. What could have changed me? I think it was when I started to take trading seriously, when I got tired of losing, going through emotional lifts, feeling like the master of the world on Monday and being on the verge of suicide on Friday, when I realized that no one predicts the future and that the stock market is simply rhythmic in the end.

Prices breathe, they are tossed up and down by a form of group unconsciousness. People are optimistic, the financial markets go through the roof. People are pessimistic, the financial markets crash excessively. It's nothing more and nothing less than excess to trade. Waiting for excess and watching what it does on a pivot point for example. Is it coming back up? I buy. Has it broken? What is the next pivot point where it might stop falling? Just a game of movement that is not at all random because when you study the charts precisely, you realize that there are recurrences.

Trigger number two

I was wasting time trying to move too fast. I did not respect the necessary stages of progression. You don't go from €5 per point to €25 per point on the Dax 30 even if its capital has multiplied by five. It's not the same trading at all, the same tension. You have to take your time, climb gradually in stages and when you feel comfortable at one stage go to the next stage up. And don't set limits, the first cause of our failures is ourselves. We impose glass ceilings on ourselves. For example, I see novice traders coming in and saying, "it's impossible to win on the financial markets". They put themselves in a position of instant failure.

Trigger number three

We all have invisible glass ceilings.

To illustrate this statement, I will give you two examples.

I couldn't break the €100,000 mark on the financial markets. I used to trade well and as soon as I got close to that symbolic 6-figure level, I would do something stupid and get a slap in the face. And this happened to me not once but 12 times in a row. I was able to identify this through my trading journal. Why was it that when I got close to this amount, I would eventually do everything I could to plummet? It was an unconscious reaction related to my father.

My father is a labourer who has always had two or three jobs at the same time, a slave working six days a week at least. After a lifetime of hard work, he managed to save €100,000 to retire. Having very high esteem for my father, I couldn't get any more money than him as a youngster of 30. It was like disrespecting him. When I realized that, that I could have more money than him at 30, without it devaluing his working life, I freed myself to progress.

Another example is the use of invisible glass ceilings. I knew a brilliant person, a respected and recognized engineer, high schools all the blah blah. And he was a very good trader. So much so that he made more money trading than he did going to work. He therefore logically asked himself why not stop going to work, especially since he no longer enjoyed it. We were talking, and I could feel his stress. Logic dictated that he should stop, but he was also afraid of losing his social status as an engineer, that other people's outlook would change, etc. What do you think happened?

Inevitably, although he had been trading very well for years, he made a huge blunder, he got a monumental slap in the face. And that relieved him, he unconsciously caused this. He no longer had to make the difficult decision that haunted him, it was no longer relevant. He had to remain an engineer and maintain his social status. He'd managed to get his tension under control.

By working on yourself, by analysing yourself, you will have one or more triggers that will change everything in your trading and your life. That's the best I can wish for you.

47

THE TRANSITION TO PROPRIETARY TRADING

As we saw with the example of the engineer who was unable to take the step to radically change his life, the transition to professional trading is far from being psychologically obvious.

When I was a teacher, I spent my evenings trading the Nasdaq 100 out of passion but also in the hope one day to leave National Education. Effectively, the day I realized that my life was all mapped out, that I was able to calculate my retirement to the nearest penny at the age of 30, I became afraid. I felt like I was already dead and had no future.

My life was already mapped out, I was going to marry a teacher, we would have two children, a house in the suburbs, certainly a Labrador, we'd call him Max, etc. Being single and having no children, I didn't care about my title of teacher, I risked absolutely nothing to embark on the adventure of trading on my own account. At worst, I would have done something else, I would have looked for a job as a teacher in the private sector. On the other hand, if I had had children, I would never have dragged other people into my adventure, I would have remained a teacher.

Looking back, I think my decision was not rational but impulsive. I'm not encouraging anyone to do that. The last thing you should do is quit. It would have been a lot smarter to put myself on a part-time basis, for example, to continue teaching and trading two to three days a week in a professional manner. I could have had a transition period of a few years to consolidate my trading and not be under pressure.

Becoming a proprietary trader is indeed very complicated psychologically. Beyond the pressure, you can quickly find yourself socially isolated. A trader on his own account lives out of step with the rest of the population. Our schedules are peculiar if we trade the American markets for example.

The degraded social image of this activity must also be considered. I won't go into details, my book "Traders are True Communists" is devoted solely to this theme. I know proprietary traders who would rather tell their neighbours that they are graphic designers than admit the "horrible" truth. This form of social pressure, which can be very burdensome in the long run, must also be considered.

But in the end, I think we should neither idealize nor be afraid of this activity. An executive who resigns to open a bed and breakfast or a restaurant also takes risks. It's the unknown that's scary. We know what we're leaving but we don't know what we're going to find.

So it is, in fact, the issue of change that is at the heart, the activity in itself is no more risky or complicated than creating a new business in a lambda activity.

Since we're talking about psychology, there's something I never would have thought of before. You can be afraid of losing money in trading and this is one of the reasons why you can't manage to cash in your losses (because the losses are validated and recorded, there is no more "hope", hence the danger of going into "hope" mode, which often turns into "despair" mode).

But you can also be afraid of making money. That is to say that when your position is progressing extremely well, you cash in your gains, not because there is a turnaround, but because the tension is just as strong as when you lose money. So, we sabotage ourselves by cashing in our position in mid-stream. Not even having the reflex to put a TP +XX to ensure a gain, you want to get out because gains (like losses) are unbearable in terms of tension. And by cutting the position, you also cut the tension.

This may sound crazy to you, but at least that's what I've been going through for a while. I had in my heart this Judeo-Christianity that society was sending me back to my roots and the fact that I came from a working-class background. I was a farm labourer for a few months, a market vendor, market porter, etc. I know what it's like to do hard work to earn a small salary. And sitting at my desk for a few hours I could earn much more. I think that if I had come from an aristocratic or bourgeois background, the question wouldn't have arisen, earning so much money would have been natural.

That's what's so exciting about trading, the more you progress, the newer doors open up that you weren't even aware of. When I was a teacher, I was convinced that the day I would earn money regularly on the stock market everything would be simple. The good life.

Well no, not at all, other problems arise, other psychological challenges to overcome. The adventure continues!

EPILOGUE

The middle of the road

It's already time to say goodbye after more than 400 pages. Time has gone by so fast and I wish I could tell you more, but I also know when to stop and let apprentice traders find their own way.

I hope that this book gives you ideas to develop or rectify your trading, raises questions for those who know and I hope that it may have contributed, or will contribute in a few years, to a trigger like I was lucky enough to have.

I'm writing this epilogue at a time when the Andlil.com forum has just exceeded the symbolic level of 1,000,000 messages. I invite you to join it, we can meet there, I would be pleased to answer your questions. Don't forget that you have access to the private part of the site with videos and updates to keep this book up to date and alive always.

You have decided, by buying this book, to make progress in your trading. I have spent an enormous amount of time pointing out the dangers, the efforts to be made and the difficulties you will encounter along this path.

I wouldn't like to leave you with this feeling without telling you that trading is also and above all fun, an everyday joy, a passion that is constantly renewed. It's impossible to get bored while trading, there's always something going on.

Trading also gives you a lot, and I'm not talking about that feeling of freedom to be able to live anywhere, to be able to trade wherever we want, to have no hierarchy or accountability except to ourselves. No, when I say that trading gives you a lot it is that it helps us to discover ourselves, to progress, to become adults.

If you've only recently discovered trading, know that you've just opened the door to an incredible world that can transform you completely.

You will no longer see the world with the same eyes, and you will experience an incredible passion that will go far beyond the money earned.

There are poetry and aestheticism in the act of trading. and I wish, from the bottom of my heart, that you live and feel that.

Benoist Rousseau

ANNEX

Do you want some more?

One last little trade before we part ways.

Stock Market Proverbs

There are a few financial market proverbs that I find very meaningful and that you should know, especially if you are new to the financial markets. These are sayings that all have some truth in them. Overall, they all call for doubt and caution.

A bird in the hand is worth two in the bush.

This is not a stock market proverb, but it is full of common sense and it is my favourite. This is even the basis of my trading, knowing how to take profits before my position falls into the red. It's better to secure a profit than to get slapped in the face in the stock market. The number of times I got caught -XXXX € at the end of the day when I was at +XXXX € taught me to respect this stock market adage. You mustn't be greedy and eager in the stock market.

You have to know how to cash in your positions. The use of a stop profit to guarantee a profit is the best way to give a winning position its "chance" while taking no more risk. The use of a guaranteed stop for swing trading is a good example.

Buy the rumour and sell the news.

Rumours lead to price increases, once the rumour is confirmed the rise stops. It is, therefore, a good idea to buy when the rumour breaks and sell when the news is confirmed.

You can see that this stock market proverb works very often. This can be explained by the group unconscious that governs the stock markets. Man is often disappointed when he reaches the object and this saying reminds us of that.

Buy to the sound of a cannon and sell to the sound of a bugler.

It is better to buy when the economic situation is bad because the prices are low and to sell when the prices have risen, i.e. when the situation has improved.

A similar proverb says: bullish markets are born in pessimism, grow in scepticism and die in euphoria.

Trees don't grow right up to the sky; the stock exchange is made of the same wood.

Prices cannot constantly rise. Historically, prices always reach a resistance and suffer a downturn at some point.

Favour daughters over mothers.

In times of economic turbulence and turmoil, it is less risky to invest in a subsidiary than in a parent company. Indeed, a parent company will normally be more affected in the event of a crisis.

When Wall Street sneezes, the Paris stock exchange catches a cold.

The American position on the financial markets is so large that its fluctuations directly affect smaller markets such as the Paris stock exchange.

A very important adage to remember, reminding us that it's the U.S. stock markets that make it rain and shine.

In the morning the European markets are "autonomous", then they wait for the opening of the American markets (lower volatility in the early afternoon). Then, they generally pass on changes in the U.S. indices in their prices from 3.30 pm onwards.

Therefore, you have to trade the European indices in the afternoon with a constant look at the major U.S. indices. If we don't, we're trading blind.

It's when there are blue skies that thunderstorms break out.

It's always when you least expect them that the cracks come. When the subprime crisis erupted, the New York Stock Exchange had been rising steadily since 2003.

It's better to cut off your hand now than cut off your arm later.

You need to know how to place stop losses and minimize your losses when a position is unfavourable. This adage is very popular with professional traders but less so with individuals who find it difficult to close negative positions. And they sink.

Never hunt down the last euro.

You should not be too "greedy", if you have a very favourable position, you should not try to reach absolutely the highest level to sell, even if opinions remain positive.

You have to know how to cash in your winnings and not want too much. In the 2000s, I knew individuals who were virtually millionaires and would have been if they had sold their shares, but they lost everything. The Alcatel share, for example, went from €100 to €2.

The market burns what it loved in the past.

Financial markets have a trend of creating speculative bubbles by excessively favouring one sector. These bubbles can then burst, with the consequences we all know.

You will not improve your results by pulling flowers and watering weeds.

A prudent investor should, at most, let his profits run and close his unfavourable positions as quickly as possible. To do this you need to place stop losses close to the price and profit stops further away to give the position a chance to advance.
Don’t catch a falling knife.

You should not invest in a security that falls in a normal economic situation. If the security price falls for no reason, its price is unstable, so beware of the sharp edge.

This adage is important during violent stock market crashes and downturns. A lot of people seeing the low prices are tempted to buy. And they try for a second bearish wave. In the case of a sharp drop, you should never anticipate the rebound but accompany it when it forms and protect it with a stop profit as soon as possible.

Don't put all your eggs in one basket.

By diversifying your portfolio, you may have a lower rate of return, but in the event of a stock market crash, you minimize your losses. Caution, caution.

Never follow others like sheep, sheep get sheared.

Blindly following investor majorities is not always a good idea, you can miss out on good investments or follow a trend that goes straight to the wall. This is in line with the rule of trading, think for yourself.

TABLE OF CONTENTS

A word from the Author 11

THE BASICS OF TRADING

The start of the journey 15

1 TRADER, IT'S A PROFESSION 17

2 IS TRADING INNATE OR CAN IT BE LEARNED? 21

3 THE IMPORTANCE OF PAPER TRADING WHEN YOU BEGIN 25

4 THE IMPORTANCE OF TRADING JOURNALS.................... 31

5 TRADING, THE QUEST FOR PERFECTION 39

6 WHICH BROKER TO CHOOSE?.. 43

7 HOW TO CHOOSE A TRADING STATION 49

8 OPTIMIZE AND SECURE YOUR TRADING STATION........... 57

9 WHY TRADE INDICES?.. 63

10 UNDERSTANDING FUTURES.. 69

11 HOW TO CALCULATE YOUR LEVERAGE 75

12 ECONOMIC CONCEPTS AND THE PACE OF FINANCIAL MARKETS 79

13 I DON'T UNDERSTAND ANYTHING ABOUT THE FINANCIAL MARKETS! 87

14 REVIEW 93

MY TRADING METHOD

Research.. 97

15 HOW TO FIND YOUR OWN TRADING METHOD 99

16 MY TRADING STATION CHARTS 111

17 A SCALPER IS A SNIPER 119

18 WHICH INDICES TO CHOOSE FOR SCALPING AND DAY TRADING 129

19 MY TRADING INDICATORS 133

20 HEIKIN ASHI AND DOW'S LAW 151

21 SCALPING PIVOT POINTS 159

22 SCALPING SYMBOLIC LEVELS 169

23 RANGE TRADING 175

24 BREAKOUT TRADING 179

25 TAKE YOUR LOSSES: MILITARY TECHNIQUE 183

26 ON WHICH DAYS SHOULD TRADING BE AVOIDED? 189

27 WHY FRIDAY IS SPECIAL ON THE STOCK MARKET 195

28 EVALUATING TRADING QUALITY 199

29 ANNUITY OR ACCUMULATION TRADING 207

MY MONEY MANAGEMENT, RULES AND RITUALS

Persevere 213

30 CREATING THE FRAMEWORK 215

31 MONEY MANAGEMENT, THE ART OF SURVIVAL 219

32 THE TRADER'S MANTRA 225

Back to work! 229

33 RULE NUMBER 1: DON'T LOSE ANY MONEY 231

34 RULE NUMBER 2: REREAD RULE NUMBER 1 235

35 RULE NUMBER 3: ONLY TRADE WHEN FIT 239

36 RULE NUMBER 4: DO NOT BE SWAYED 243

37 RULE NUMBER 5: CONTROL YOUR LOSSES: 247

38 RULE NUMBER 6: DO NOT FORCE YOURSELF TO TRADE 255

39 RULE NUMBER 7: BREAK THE NORMAL RULES 261

40 THE TRADER'S RITUAL 265

THE PSYCHOLOGY OF TRADING

Suffer 275

41 THE CRUELTY OF REALITY 277

42 STRESS IN TRADING 283

43 FRUSTRATION IN TRADING 289

44 THE PROTECTION SHIELD AND TRADING 293

45 GRIEF IN TRADING 299

46 STRENGTHENING AND PSYCHOLOGICAL TRIGGERS..... 305

47 THE TRANSITION TO PROPRIETARY TRADING............. 315

EPILOGUE

The middle of the road 319

ANNEX

Stock Market Proverbs 323

www.ingramcontent.com/pod-product-compliance
Lightning Source LLC
Chambersburg PA
CBHW071426230926
51846CB00001B/129